C 8 *The Author*

(Photograph: B.R.Jones)

Yours sincerely
Joe Newell
19th March 1991.

The
Holywell Story

by

Joe Newell

Published for the Author

by

Graham-Cameron Publishing, Cambridge, England

 ISBN 0 94767 221 4

For Eileen

Who shared the wonder –
the joy – and the tears

Acknowledgements

The author would like to thank the following people, whose kindness to him during the compilation and writing of this book made the task considerably easier and more pleasant. Bob Burns-Murdoch, Curator of the Norris Library and Museum St. Ives for his ever willing assistance, Alan Neale for his photograph of the Trinity Foot Beagles. Philip Reeson of Ewing-Reeson and Brian Jones for their photographic work. The Cambridge University Collection of Aerial Photography. Sarah Colegrave of Sothebys, London. Lesley James and the County Record Office. Mike and Helen Graham-Cameron for editing and co-ordinating the final production.

The chapter on 'The Artists of Holywell' is based on research work by Michael Knight, and the personal records of Andrew Baird Grove.

My thanks are due to Ken Walton for allowing me to use his drawings on pages i, 41, 51, 79, 93 and 157, and to Bob Burns-Murdoch for the drawings on pages 1, 45 and 68.

Lastly, but by no means least, special thanks to Fay Richardson without whose encouragement the Holywell Story might never have been written.

St. Ives

1991

Joe Newell

Contents

Part 1 • Holywell through the Ages

Part 2 • A Childhood Remembered

Appendices •

Part 1

Holywell through the Ages

Chapter 1

The Village

Here Ouse,
slowly wending through a level plain
of spacious meads,
with cattle sprinkled o'er,
Conducts the eye along
it's sinuous course
Delighted.

William Cowper.

Ten Thousand Years ago, toward the end of the Old Stone Age, warm weather began to melt the Ice Age Snows and by 5500 B.C. England was an island. Until then our own river Ouse was a tributary of the great Rhine river which carried waters through the land mass of Europe and out to the northern seas by the southern coast of Norway. Around 3000 B.C. that part of East Anglia which we know as the Fens began to flood, and by 1000 B.C. the Isle of Ely had been formed.

River Ouse at Holywell

The waters encroached inland to the very edge of Peterborough and Cambridge, and along the river Ouse valley, only then being held back by the higher ground. It must have been a worrying time for those early growers of grain and raisers of cattle. Here on the very edge of the fen it may safely be assumed that an early stone age tribe founded a settlement which as the centuries passed became the village of Holywell.

The village is situated about one and a half miles eastward of St. Ives across the meadows by the public footpath. By road it is about three miles through the village of Needingworth with which it forms the Parish of Holywell-cum-Needingworth. The two settlements were joined, and still are, by a road running north and south through the centre of the old common field, named Mill Road.

The habitations of the village lie along two roads running irregularly east and west, which are connected at each end. The northern road is called Black Lane and the southern Holywell Front. The Church is at the west end of the southern road, east of it is the 'old' rectory and nearby the 'new' rectory. In Conger Lane at the western juncture of the two roads is the Manor House, and along both roads are picturesque timber framed cottages.

Several of the houses in the village date from the 17th century some of them built by dutch settlers who first came to the fens as prisoners of war from naval battles, and joined the Scottish prisoners from the battle of Dunbar, to carry out the labouring work connected with the drainage of the fens. Under instruction of that famous Dutch Engineer Vermuyden their work made thousands of acres of land available for cultivation and led to the area being known as the bread basket of England. Many families in the fens owe their ancestry to these settlers.

The village derives it's name from a spring of soft water rising near the bottom of the hill on which the church stands. Not far away across the rector's field the quiet Ouse wends it's onward way toward the sea, catching at eventide the colours of the setting sun. A scene much loved by many artists who have set up their easels here in an endeavour to capture in water colour and oil the ever changing pattern and shades of the wide fen sky.

The name Holywell was given to the district around the well many years before the growth of Needingworth. It is thought that the name arose in Roman times, from use of the water for sacred purposes - it really is a spring and not a 'well' at all. In some old papers the name is given as Halliewelle or Holie-welle, spelled in various ways. It was not until the 18th century that Holywell became the generally accepted way of spelling the village name.

According to legend the well owes it's reputed sanctity to the seventh century Persian Bishop Ivo who was buried at St. Ives and whose remains were transferred to Ramsey Abbey about 1000 A.D. His bones, and wells and springs connected with his name were credited with healing properties. As recently at 1933 a woman was seen sitting with her feet in the water to cure a foot complaint. People often came to bathe for such complaints as sore eyes. In 1934 a boy was reported to have been healed of a sore on his forehead after bathing it with water from the well, the remedy having been tried as a last resort. The water is now considered unfit for human or animal consumption. In my youth water cress grew abundantly in the clear gravel bed of the outflow, and in the spring of the year this was gathered by villagers for their own use, and by myself to be sold to greengrocers in St. Ives, as a valuable source of pocket money. The flow of water was much greater then than it now is.

Many summer visitors to the village mistakenly regard it as a Wishing Well and throw coins in the water, to some small benefit of Church income. In 1845 the basin of the 'well' was restored and surmounted by a brick canopy resembling in shape a Victorian Poke Bonnet, a brass plate carries this inscription:-

Erected by the Rev. S.B. Beckwith, Rector of this Parish A.D. 1845

This canopy has recently been rebuilt, incorporating the original brass plate, and the area around the well improved by paving.

Goodyers

In 'The Geology of the Neighbourhood of Cambridge' the authors remark that: '...the gravels where resting on clay, are of course, water bearing, and they supply most of the towns and villages situated upon or near them... But one fails to see why so much should have been made of these springs, where through some local condition of the beds, water that has percolated through the sand and gravel of a graveyard

The Friars

Berry House

The Pantiles

Hill Farm

is thrown out... The water is thrown out at a junction of the Oxford Clay with gravel in a low corner of the Churchyard at Holywell.'

The Geologist wonders why so much should have been made of the outflow of spring water at this point! However, a regular supply of clear water has always been a basic need and of paramount importance to the human race, and the water at this point was flowing thousands of years before a Church and graveyard stood on this hill. To the early wandering tribesmen and stone age settlers this area with it's high ground and constant source of life giving water would have been an ideal site to make camp, and it's continuous flowing from the ground a source of wonder and doubtless of pagan worship rites. Here then, with the coming of Christianity was the ideal place to build a Church to nurture the spirit alongside the spring which nurtured the body.

The most famous Fenland hero was Hereward the Wake, who in 1067 rallied the English resistance against William the Conqueror. Hereward converted Ely Abbey into a fortress and it was not until 1071 that it fell to the Norman invaders. Said to be through the treachery of some of it's defenders who showed the Normans a secret path through the fenland swamps in return for an amnesty.

Holywell is mentioned in his famous book 'Hereward the Wake' by Charles Kingsley. Hereward had been to Brandon to the Kings Camp a distance of 50 miles, and after playing the potter there rode home to Ely. Kingsley in describing the celebrated journey writes:-

"And he entered the forest at Madingley, he rose in his stirrups, with a shout of 'A Wake! A Wake!' which could be heard for aught he cared in Cambridge Castle: and then rode on leisurely toward the Draytons, and the ferry over the Ouse at Holywell: for well he knew that they who could not catch the Wake in the field, were still less likely to catch him in the wood."

It is more than likely that The Wake visited the Inn which stood on the site of the present Ferry Boat.

Another old legend of Holywell says:-

'There's not in this county but heard tell
of the spring near St. Ives that is called Holywell
Since the reign of King Edward this spring
has been famous,
By the powers above!
You may here see your love,
For they say it's been charmed since the days
of McManus.'

The Brook, Holywell
(R. Winter: Sothebys)

The brook which flows along the front of the village and joins the river by 'the swamp' is not known by any particular name, although one of it's northern tributaries appears to have been known at one time as the King's dyke. The source of this brook is on the high ground that is part of Wyton Airfield. It started life as a spring feeding the pond at Wyton Hill farm, now no more than a clump of trees by the Huntingdon - Warboys road: from this point it followed the lie of the land eastward across the airfield and under the old St. Ives - Oldhurst Road, then by Wiggin Hill Farm, through Marley Gap and alongside the Somersham Road to the Bramley Garage roundabout. Then under the Needingworth Road and alongside Parsons Drove to the south of Conger Lane and along Holywell front to the river. It had two tributaries also starting on the airfield, the largest being at Rectory Farm which has also been taken into the airfield. All three have been replaced by underground channels to the airfield perimeter. The common eel is known to travel overland from one stream to another, and when the brook was first channelled underground on the airfield many eels following their instinct travelled over the grass to reach the pond at Wyton Hill Farm and many were taken by workers for culinary purposes.

Tradition says that upon the hill on which the Church stands there formerly stood a lighthouse, or a beacon which gave light, and was a guide to navigators who then travelled over the black waters of the fens in their skiffs or barks, for just below the Church the land is very flat and was once entirely covered by water, this area is still known as Holywell Fen. Even now with all the improvements in river flood control these meadows are frequently inundated.

Winter time is still the dangerous period for floods. A heavy general snowfall melting quickly can pour vast quantities of water into the river systems of the Midlands and East Anglia and combined with high tides and possibly high winds can put tremendous strain on the fen drains and river banks.

Flaggholme, Holywell (R.W. Fraser: Sothebys)

The large meadow which lies between the front of the village and the river retains the name 'Flaggholme'. (Little Flaggholme next to the brook, Big Flaggholme, and beyond the flood dyke 'Twenty Pence Piece') The name may mean that there was some kind of signal and harbour for boats at Holywell, or, abounding with flag plants which are still plentiful. 'Holme' is a river island - flat land lying along a river, and occasionally covered by it's waters. Centuries ago the river had a different course, to the north of the Ouse, traces of the old river can still be seen as a hollow track and fields thereabouts are known as 'the lakes'. Until re-alignment of the counties the river formed the boundary between Huntingdonshire and Cambridgeshire.

There was probably a Roman Post or even a Fort at Holywell. Various fragments of pottery etc. have been dug up both to the east and west of the Church and identified as of Roman origin. in my schooldays I found a shard of pottery in the scrapings of a rabbit burrow on the hill below Manor farm, and this was later confirmed to be of Roman origin. The Romans had a line of forts on the Ouse - at Sandy, Eynesbury, and Godmanchester. When standing by the Church the Roman Road Via Devana, which passes through Cambridge and on to Godmanchester can clearly be seen across the fen. The high ground would be well suited for defence and it is quite likely that fords both down and upstream of Holywell were usable at that time. The Romans frequently made use of fords to cross unless it was absolutely necessary to build a bridge.

Butt beaker, late Iron Age (perhaps c 50AD) found at Holywell (Photo: B.R. Jones)

Romano-British jar of brownware, 2nd Century AD, dredged from the Ouse at Holywell (Photo: B.R. Jones)

About a mile upstream of the Ferry Boat Inn a stretch of water is known as 'the shallows' and in the 1930's it was possible to wade across at that point. The crossing frequently being used for movement of cattle between pastures on either side of the river.

In the mid 14th century the average Englishman could expect to live only to the age of 38 years. Medical science was in it's infancy, surgery was primitive, and hygiene an almost unknown word. In June of the year 1348 two merchant ships arrived at Weymouth in Dorset from the continent and brought the dreaded Bubonic Plague to England. Often referred to as the Black Death because the whole body turned black as the disease reached its final stages. Fifty thousand victims were buried in London's Spittle Croft cemetery, and as the disease spread throughout the country there was no safe haven, whole families were wiped out, and towns and villages decimated. It has been estimated that one third of England's population of three million fell victim to the disease. The plague struck Holywell during the winter and spring of 1349. There were 65 families living in the village in 1320 and by the year 1360 these had been reduced to 53. There were, of course, other diseases to contend with but the plague may well have wiped out 6 or more families and brought death to many others. The disease was not finally eradicated from England until the year 1666 and the Great Fire of London.

Hand-axe of brown flint, perhaps 200,000 years old, Old Stone Age, found at Holywell (Photo: B.R. Jones)

In the summer of 1588, all England awaited the long prepared blow of the Spanish Armada, for three years Philip II of Spain had been building a fleet which would bring his heretical enemies to their knees, for such was his intention. On May the 20th 1588 the mightiest fleet the world had yet seen set sail from Lisbon. Beacons had been prepared along the South Coast of England, the fires were kindled and soon blazed one after the other to give warning of the approaching foe. The clash between Protestant England and Catholic Spain was about to take place. According to legend Sir Francis Drake, Vice Admiral of the British Fleet, on being told the news, turned from his game of bowls on Plymouth Hoe and said 'let them wait, there is time for our game, and to beat the Spaniards after'. Mighty Spain was beaten by a combination of seamanship and adverse weather conditions. A hundred British sailors died at the hands of the Spanish, but when the fleet returned to port disease spread through the ships and thousands dies of the plague.

The part Holywell played in this epic battle was to send a contingent of six men, three with qualivers, two with pikes and one with a musket to Tilbury - 'to help repel the Spanish'. Two villagers also contributed £25 each. These men were part of a contingent from Huntingdonshire under the command of Oliver Cromwell, an Uncle of the Protector. Whether or not all six returned safely to the village is not recorded. One of the qualiver bearers was John Ibbott; his direct descendants Betty and Dorothy Ibbott are mentioned elsewhere in these pages

An important day in the country calendar is 12th night, or Old Christmas Eve January 5th, when we take down our decorations and the twelve days of merrymaking and visiting between friends comes to an end. The next day January 6th is Epiphany symbolising the revealing of the Christ child to the Three Wise Men, and the recommencement of work in the fields by the plough-men. The following Monday is known as Plough Monday. In catholic times the ploughmen kept a light burning before certain images in the Church to obtain a blessing on their work, and it was their custom to go about the neighbouring homesteads to collect money for the 'plough lights' as they were called. The candles came to an end with the Reformation, but the festival continued - the money was still collected but instead of spending it on candles it was spent on conviviality in the local tavern!

At Holywell the custom of drawing a plough round the village and threatening to plough up the doorstep of anyone refusing to pay up was continued in to the 1930's. Sometimes a boy would dress up as a girl and there would be dancing and prancing about as they shouted 'Spare a penny for the poor plough boy' or 'Please spare one, poor old plough boy ain't got none'. With blackened faces and by candle lantern it had all the elements of play acting. The Tabbitt boys were probably the last to perform this old ritual at Holywell, and Sid Tabbitt tells me that thirty shillings was reckoned to be a good collection for the evenings activity. It may not seem much by today's equivalent, especially when divided between 7 to 10 boys, but it put money in pockets that might otherwise have been empty.

Chapter 2

The Parish Church of St John the Baptist

I said to the man who stood at the gate of the year
'Give me a light that I may tread safely into the unknown'.
And he replied. "Go out into the darkness and put your
hand into the hand of God. That shall be better to you
than a light and safer than a known way!"
So I went forth and finding the hand of God,
trod gladly into the night.
And he led me toward the hills
and the breaking of day in the lone East.

M.L. Haskins 1875-1957

St. John the Baptist
Holywell Church

In the year 969, Ethelwine, Earl of East Anglia, at the instigation of Oswald, Archbishop of York, founded the convent of Ramsey for a body of Benedictine monks. The endowments of the monastery included many Parish Churches in Huntingdonshire and elsewhere. Among them was Haliwelle Church, given by Alfwara, a noble Saxon Lady, and the Manor of Nidingworth which Oswald bought from King Edgar.

This evidence shows that there was a Church well established at Holywell in 969, and therefore, probably for a considerable time before this date. The name of only one incumbent has survived, Gode, who flourished about 990. It was he who at his death left the advowson (i.e. the right of presentation to a benefice) of Holywell to the Abbot of Ramsey. After him there is a gap in the list of incumbents to 1216, at which date the Church was dedicated to St. John the Baptist. One incumbent of Holywell became Archbishop of Canterbury, Thomas Tenison, 1695 -1715.

In the Domesday Survey it is recorded that 'In Haliewell the Abbot of Ramsey has 9 Hides (1080 acres) which paid Geld (Landtax) ...here is a Church and a Priest and 3 acres of meadow. There is a wood for pannage', (for feeding pigs) 'approximately one and a quarter miles by one mile in area'. This wood was probably situated on Needingworth Heath, a ridge of high ground running roughly East to West just to the north of the old St. Ives to Bluntisham railway track. Old maps show that a 'road' or drovage led from alongside Holywell Manor house, across the common land in a direct line to the foot of Pound Hill, Needingworth where it continued as Lowndes Drove.

'There is a marsh one mile long and one broad'. This is shown on modern Ordnance Survey maps as stretching north west from the Church towards St. Ives. Earlier but unreliable maps show it around the Ferry Boat Inn. 'At the time of King Edward (The Confessor) the value was £8 and is so now...' There are very few parishes in England which did not have a Church at the time of the Norman Conquest. The date of a building may be determined by two forms of evidence, namely, documentary and architectural. The first of these, which is often wanting, can fortunately be applied to Holywell Church by the endowment of Ramsey. Architecturally, no part of the present building is earlier than the end of the 12th century: though the Victoria History of the County advances the date of the building by half a century. The two windows on the North and South Sides of the Chancel are late Norman or early Transitional in style, and the date of the Chancel depends on the dates covered by this period.

The earlier Church, most likely built of daub and wattle with a reed thatched roof, would have consisted of one room, and eventually became too small or too decrepit for the needs of the Parish and was pulled down to make room for the present structure. During repairs to the Chancel a human lower jaw bone was found in the rubble between the inner and outer walls, and no doubt came from the cemetery of the previous Church, over part of which the foundations of the present Church were built.

The Church consists of a Chancel, a Nave with North and South Aisles, a West Tower, a Vestry and South Porch.

St. John the Baptist
South Porch

The Chancel (32 feet by 16 feet) is built of stone rubble. On the South Side are two windows composed of double lancets under a semi-circular arch, the lights divided inside by a circular shaft with moulded cap and base. On the North side are two similar windows, but that on the north west has had its central portion restored (1862) to replace a 'churchwarden' window with a wooden frame. Running round the Chancel at the level of the window-sills is a plain internal string course. On the South Side is the original doorway now opening into a modern Vestry built in 1862, and re-built in 1919.

Within the Sanctuary is the original Aumbry with a modern door, and on the South Side an unusually large recessed Picena with large trefoil drain and credence. Owing to raising of the floor level it now appears rather low.

The Choir-Stalls are modern (1862) and the single manual organ was presented in 1891 by a former Rector, The Rev. H.C.W. Hoskyns as a thank offering for a narrow escape from death.

On the South wall are two mural tablets:-

1. The Rev. H. Parratt Prebendary of Lincoln and Rector 1722 - 1757, erected in 1759, and Catherine (Halford) his wife.
2. The Rev. S. Spencer, a son of a former occupant of the Manor Farm, died 1909.

On the North wall:-

1. The Rev. J. Lowry, Curate in Charge for 22 years, and Rector of

Waddeston, Bucks, died 1859. Eliza, his wife, died 1854, and two daughters Emma and Jemima, died 1842.

2. Thos. Howard, a Needingworth Parishioner who occupied a box pew in the Chancel, died 1808, Rebecca his wife, died 1815, and John Thorp Howard, their Grandson, died 1825.

The roof was retiled in 1919. The Oak Reredos with figures of the four Evangelists was erected to the Memory of John Bolding Ellis, a former Churchwarden, who died in 1915, underneath is a richly carved communion table to the memory of the above and his wife, Susan Jane, died 1921, added in 1922. With the exception of the sill and inner jambs the East Window was entirely renewed in 1862. The stained glass, which is by Nicholson, was inserted in 1931.

The central figure represents Our Lord in regal and priestly garments. His right hand uplifted in blessing, and His left holds a sceptre on which is an emblem of the Trinity, underneath is a scene at the supper at Emmaus.

On the left is a large figure of Edmund, King and Martyr, the last of the Kings of East Anglia killed by the Danes in 870, and below is a scene of his martyrdom.

On the right is a large figure of Oswald Archbishop of York and Bishop of Worcester. His right hand holds an archiepiscopal cross and his left a model of Worcester Cathedral which he refounded. On the top is the arms of York Impaling Oswald, half way on the left side is the Arms of Worcester impaling Oswald, and underneath an imaginary scene in which Oswald presents the deeds of the Manor of Needingworth, which he bought from King Edgar, to the first Abbot of Ramsey in 969, in the presence of King Edgar, the Lady Alfwara and Ethelwine, Earl of East Anglia. In the three small lights above on the left is the emblem of St. John the Baptist, viz. a pascal lamb standing on a book, on the right is the emblem of St. Benedict, viz. a devil issuing from a broken chalice on a book, and the topmost light contains a view of the holy well with the inscription. "Quoniam apud te est fons vitae" Ps.36, v 9. ("since with thee is the well of life").

Dividing the nave from the Chancel is a modern oak screen in the 15th century style, erected in 1923 to the memory of William Ross, father of a previous incumbent, the Rev J.A. Ross. It has the following inscription carved in old lettering "William Ross, obit 2nd Augt 1918 anno aetatis sui LXIV: cujus animae propitietur Deus. Amen". This screen replaces a medieval one removed in 1862. There are six Armorial Shields on the screen reading from left to right as follows:-

1. Montague (Patrons from Charles 1st to 1866)
2. Ramsey Abbey (Patrons 969 to 1539)
3. James Alfred Ross (Rector 1914 to 1945)
4. Diocese of Ely
5. Diocese of Lincoln (Until 1836 Huntingdonshire was in this Diocese)
6. Province of Canterbury.

The nave, which is 38 ft by 16 ft., has a North arcade of 13th century date, consisting of three bays with pointed arches and octagonal columns. The lower order at the West end is carried on a moulded corbel supported on a carved head. At the east end of the North aisle is a two light window distorted in shape owing to settlements, and a 13th century North doorway between two windows dating from the restoration of 1862. Here no doubt stood the Chantry abolished in 1551. The doorway leading to the rood loft staircase and the staircase itself have disappeared, but the rood loft doorway, which was blocked up an plastered over in 1862 was re-opened in 1919. The clerestory on both North and South sides has three two light early 16th century windows. The South arcade, of early 14th century, is also of three bays of similar design to that on the North. The centre arch is higher and wider than the others. The lower order at the West end, as with the North arcade, is carried on a moulded corbel supported on a carved head. At the East end of the South aisle is a 14th century three light window which has also become distorted through subsidence. The South doorway is also 14th century. The carved stone bosses supporting the roof are medieval, and one of these facing the South door has a "Jack in the Green". In the East window of the South aisle there are shields, inserted about 1925 representing incumbents of the 16th and 17th centuries.

1. Trinity Hall, Cambridge, Impaling Walter Hewke (on top)
2. Trinity Hall, Cambridge, Impaling William Dallyng (top right hand)
3. Queens' College, Cambridge. (William Chaderton, President 1568-79)
4. Diocese of Lincoln, Impaling William Chaderton.
5. Diocese of Chester, Impaling William Downham.

6. Corpus Christi College, Cambridge. Impaling Francis Wilford.
7. Deanery of Ely, Impaling Francis Wilford.
8. Province of Canterbury, Impaling Thomas Tenison. (Archbishop of Canterbury 1694-1715)

The West tower is in three stages with angle buttresses, and has an embattled parapet with crocketed pinnacles at the corners. The building of the tower was begun in 1547. Thomas Roper being the mason, and finished in 1551. It is constructed of wrought Barnack stone taken from the dissolved Abbey of Ramsey. The pyramidical roof, formerly tiles was leaded in 1929. There is a richly moulded and carved tower arch of 14th century date, supported on plain square piers; the side walls have recesses under similar arches, and the West Wall has an early 16th century doorway above which is a square-headed three light window. In the North South and West walls of the belfry are three re-used 14th century windows of two-trefoiled lights in a two-centred head. In the East wall is a square-headed light above a square-headed doorway leading out on to the roof of the Nave. The roof of the tower is reached through a trap-door, by an iron ladder from the bell-chamber. The stair turret is in the south-west angle of the tower. There is an old inscription on the interior South Wall, about 10ft. from the ground: "W.L. Clerk, 1689" i.e. William Lambert, Parish Clerk, buried 1723. The inscription, probably his own work, records the date of his appointment. John Dromyng, who was Rector from 1535 to 1543, may have begun the project for building, or rebuilding, the tower, as he left £6 for this purpose. The belfry was restored in 1915 and there are now six bells fitted with the Ellacombe chiming apparatus, inscribed as follows:-

1. Presented by the family of William Ross in memory of Eliza A. Barker, 1915. J. Alfred Ross, M.A. Rector.
2. John Peachey, John Bessel, Church Wardens 1625.
3. The Lord ivst in all his wayes, 1625.
4. When ye heare my dolefvl sound repent before ye coeme to grovnd. (and on the rim) I cal al men to Church to serve the Lord, I cal to grave and yet speake not a word. 1625.
5. Cvm cano bvsta moricvm pvlpita vivere dise (for disce).1625.
6. Presented by William Gordon Ross in memory of James Alfred Ross, Rector of Holywell, 1914 to September 1945.

This bell was cast by John Taylor and Co of Loughborough, in 1947. The same firm also re-cast and rehung in a new frame the old bells in 1915 as a gift of John Bolding Ellis, a Churchwarden. In 1552 there were three great bells. The old bells were cast by William Hausley of St. Ives. The font has a modern bowl standing on a 13th century pillar and supported by four small shafts of varying dates, with moulded caps and bases. The old box pews were replaced by oak pews in 1862, and previous to that date the Font stood near the West pier on the South side. The pulpit is modern and replaces a medieval one which stood on the South side of the Chancel arch. The brass eagle lectern was given by Reginald Mortimer to commemorate the Diamond Jubilee. There was formerly a West gallery, erected in 1561 and dismantled in 1862.

The heating apparatus was installed in 1916. The interior of the Church was entirely redecorated, and the corbels painted in 1953. Electric lighting was installed in 1946, replacing the old oil lamps, but using the chains and fitments, in memory of the Rev. J.A. Ross. The electric organ blower was fitted in 1948. A screen of English oak with clear glass panels was erected between the nave of the Church and the west tower, and dedicated by the Bishop of Huntingdon on 24th June 1983.

The Rectory, Holywell, 1930

The Mediaeval Church of England prohibited labour on festal days, and required people of all classes to attend the church services. Therefore, on these days the Church busied herself to find entertainment for the people, and thus the Holy Day became identified with the 'Holiday'. For the most part the gatherings were held in the Church-house, a building usually close by the Church. At the Church-house were held Church Ales, also Bride Ales (hence Bridal) for those too poor to provide their own wedding feast. Clerk Ales were held to find the stipend of the Parish Clerk.

There are several entries in the Holywell Church Warden's Accounts connected with the Church House. The first mention is in the year 1552. In the year 1591 it comes to be called the Town-House and the last mention is in a document dated 1679.

In the Parish Award of 1801 there is mention of a piece of land containing the site of the Town House which was apparently in Church Street, Needingworth. In 1563 there was a "Great Wynde which did much damage to both the Church at Hollywelle and the Church House".

There must have been some very jolly occasions at the Church-House and one can imagine how much they were looked forward to by the rural community. The building often consisted of an upstairs room for 'the ladies chattering', and a downstairs room for the mens' 'more serious business'.

There is one recorded instance of the flagstones of the lower floor of a Church-House hiding a cavity in which contraband liqueur was stored and sold by the Sexton on festive occasions to raise funds, this would have added to the jollity of the festival, but I can find no record of any similar occurrence at Holywell. With the coming of more enlightened times Church-Houses were sold and frequently became the Village Inn. Unfortunately, there is no record of the exact location or fate of Holywell Church-House.

In the year 1602 Noah Bowyer (or Bowier) became Rector and there arose between him and his Parishioners a dispute over the payment of tithes — a tenth of the annual produce of agriculture devoted to the support of the priesthood. On the 31st May, 1612 as a result of litigation between the Rector and his parishioners, an Arbitor was chosen who ordered that the two parties should cease their actions, each paying their own costs and that 'the said parties shall ever after live in love and unity together'.

Among the tithes awarded were:-

> *'Every parishioner having pigges to the number of seven or above to pay one tithe pigge, to be taken away when the pigges are one month old, to be chosen as follows. The owner first to choose two, and then the Parson to take the third.'*

Tithe hay to be paid as follows:

> *'The Tenth poale or forke length for the tithe laying, the tithe one year at one end, and the other year at the other end, either to be taken in swarthe ready mown. A tenth part of honey coming from the bees to be carried to the Parsonage House. Tithes on pears, apples, quinces, peaches, to be paid when the same are pulled at the tree root, and brought to the Parsonage House. Tithe eggs to be paid on Good Friday, as follows: For one cock, one drake, and one turkey cock, three eggs of every kind respectively, and for every hen, duck, and turkey, two eggs, and for the Parsonage to send for the eggs to the parishioners houses. At every drawing of the river the Parson to send bread and beer to the workmen, and the Parson to have a tenth part of the fish. Also, the parishioners, or some of them, or one of them, shall, upon the Feast of Pentecost next coming or before, pay unto Noah Bowyer the sum of four marks in the Parsonage House at Hallywelle, in token of their love and kindness toward him, and ease him of some part of the charges of the lawsuits, or otherwise the Parishioners not to pay him anything.'*

The settlement seems to have been successful to all parties, as we find Noah Bowyer still Rector until his death in 1645.

There was a Chapel of Ease dedicated to St. James at Needingworth, this was a small building with just the one altar, and existed for the worship and prayer of those who through age or infirmity could not make the journey to the mother Church at Holywell. Some would already have journeyed on foot from outlying habitations of the parish, perhaps in inclement weather, and no doubt there was a regular if small congregation. Its position is believed to have been in the field known as Chapel Close - now part of a housing development. The Chapel does not appear to have had any right of burial as parishioners directed in their Wills that they be buried at

Holywell. The Chapel is first mentioned in 1252, but seems to have fallen into disuse after the Reformation and was closed down between 1552 and 1579. In the year 1801 it was declared to be in ruins.

In the year 1526 John Gerves of Holywell at his death left to The High Altar of the Church at Holywell:

> *'To the Church 12 pence*
> *To the Chapel of Ease 6 pence*
> *I will that half a trentall be sung for me and my friends.*
> *Witness Sir Roger Reynold.*
> *In 1537 John Lambert of Holywell left to the*
> *Chapel of Ease at Needingworth 20 pence.'*

There has been no dissenting Chapel at Holywell and few dissenters from the established Church, however, the records of the Chapel at Fenstanton show that a small number of Holywell parishioners worshipped there.

> *'On 6th August 1652 Edmond Maile and Henry Browne did go to Holywell to our sister Smith, and declared to her that she had long absented herself from the Fenstanton congregation. She attended the next service on 24th." "That Joan Parker, that was servant to our Sister Smith, ran away from her service, not making her master or dame acquainted therewith. Thos. Cox and Thomas Phillips should go to her and sharply reprove her for it."*
> *"August 29.1676 William Yarle of Holliwall, Deacon of the Fenstanton Chapel 'died in the faith'*

Joseph 'Joey' Mansfield, had a lifelong connection with Holywell Church and when he died at the age of 81, a muffled peal of bells was rung to his memory. He was Churchwarden, Sexton, Bell Ringer and Gardener at the Rectory for the Rev J.A. Ross M.A. He was also Clerk to the Parish Council.

To me he was the provider of choice 'conkers' from the Rectory chestnut tree, these chestnuts were carefully laid on the ledge at the back of the kitchen range at the Manor to harden, and with them I won many a contest in the school yard.

In many Parishes the Passing Bell was rung when a person was at the point of death so that the people could offer prayer for the soul of the dying person, but at Holywell its solemn sound rang out after death had occurred. The bell tolled three times three for a man, three times two for a woman, and three for a child, followed by the number of

Joseph 'Joey' Mansfield and Mary, his wife

years the person had lived. After a pause the tolling would be repeated. The Sexton reckoned to be paid a shilling for performing this sad duty. People would stand until the count was finished and say, 'Ah!, that will be so and so', followed by reminiscences of the dead person's life. If the deceased came from Needingworth, on the day of the funeral the Church bell would commence the tolling as the cortege passed Holywell windmill. Work on the farm would stop while the cortege passed, men removed their hats, and if in the fields stood by the horse's head out of respect. There was a solemnity and pervading silence in the village, common sounds such as the lowing of cattle or the call of a wood pigeon would seem unusually noticeable. Almost always the deceased would 'belong' to the local community and his or her life would in some way, however small, have had some bearing on the life of those who now shared in the parting.

As a pupil at St. Ives Grammar School I once received 'six of the best' for not standing to attention, cap in hand, by the pathway at The Waits, St. Ives as a funeral passed by, having been observed by Captain Fraser from his study window. My excuse that I was facing the river at the time was not accepted as valid.

Each year the Church celebrates its Feast Day by a Flower Festival, and of the several organisations which take part it is the Horticultural Society that has introduced Well Dressing. The art of Well Dressing is usually associated with Derbyshire, and it was an exhibit by Bakewell at the Chelsea Flower Show of 1980 depicting 'The Lord's Supper' which inspired the Holywell-cum-Needingworth Horticultural Society to contribute a picture in flowers at the 1981 flower festival.

The dressing of the Well with a beautifully designed picture constructed entirely from natural objects such as, flower petals, leaves, moss, pebbles etc., all set in clay has now become a regular feature. The theme is usually biblical and has included 'Peace' and 'In the Beginning'. This year of 1990 the theme is 'God is Love' and has a special relevance to the Church celebrating one thousand years of continuous priesthood and service to the community at Holywell, and in addition, one hundred years since the formation of the Mothers Union movement. The 'Blessing of the well' takes place on the Friday nearest to that of the Patronal Festival, 24th June.

The Well at Holywell

Chapter 3

The Artists of Holywell

In the late nineteenth century and the early years of this century a number of artists came to live in Holywell and other riverside villages near St. Ives. For example, W. Dendy Sadler installed himself in River House, Hemingford Grey, in about 1890. The same house was subsequently the home of A.F.W. Hayward and then of Miss Greta Glynn, both notable artists. F.G. Cotman, the nephew of J.J. Cotman, lived in the village and had a studio in St. Ives. The studio was later used by W.W. Milne, who had come from Edinburgh to live in Houghton in about 1910. The American artist, Aubrey W. Hunt, lived at the Manor House, Hemingford Grey in 1903. This house, reputed to be the oldest inhabited house in England, had been the home of members of the Fraser family of artists and would later be featured by Lucy Boston in her children's books about Green Knowe. W. Kay Blacklock and his wife lived in Houghton and then in Hemingford Abbots. Charles Whymper built his house in Houghton in about 1920.

In the summer, artists from London and elsewhere would come to stay for a few weeks or months to paint the villages along the river. Scenes of old churches, riverside inns, thatched cottages and decaying watermills fitted the public demand for somewhat idealised representations of country life. Moreover, Huntingdonshire and the Fens had largely, with a few important exceptions, been ignored by artists in the earlier years of the 19th century. Accordingly, pictures of St. Ives Bridge and Houghton Mill still had some novelty value. E.M. Wimperis wrote an article in "The Leisure Hour", 1895 called "Favourite Sketching Grounds: The Hemingfords". It may be assumed that Holywell was a favourite sketching ground for many artists.

It happened that Holywell became the home of at least four artist members of the Fraser family and their wives and children. As their name suggests the Frasers were a Scottish family and claimed descent from a sister of Robert the Bruce. They came to live in Bedford, at addresses in Alexandra and Ashburnham Roads, when Robert Winchester Fraser, M.D., M.A., retired from the Army in 1860. He had been a Surgeon-Major with the 34th Foot Regiment. His father, Commander Francis Fraser, R.N., had had the distinction of being an admiral in the Portuguese navy as well as a serving officer in the

Royal Navy. He was also, by birth, the Laird of Findrack, Aberdeenshire. There were eleven children in the family, seven boys and four girls. Six of the boys became professional artists and one went into the consular service. (The family tree is shown in Appendix 1.) Of the grandchildren, two became full-time artists and another may have painted occasionally. The concentration of such talent in one family is exceptional, but not unknown.

The children who were at school in Bedford were taught painting by Bradford Rudge, art master at The Harpur School, Bedford, who, besides being a painter, also drew and lithographed views of Buckden Palace and of Buildings in Huntingdon. The Fraser boys obviously had a gift for painting and their talent was recognised early in life. The eldest son, Francis Arthur Anderson Fraser, who eventually lived in Dover, was showing his pictures in public exhibitions by the time he was 21.

White Rose Cottage
Home of A.A.F.

The third son, Robert Winchester, began to exhibit in 1874, by which time he would have been 26. In about 1884 the retired army surgeon and his wife left Bedford and moved to the Old Manor House in Hemingford Grey. Presumably, some of the children were still living with them, but George Gordon Fraser had left Bedford earlier than his parents. He first lived in Hemingford Abbots and then crossed the river by 1878 to live at the Old House, Houghton. This was about a mile away in a direct line across the water meadows from the Manor House. Also, since 1876, his elder brother, Garden William Fraser, had lived in the "House in the Fields". Hemingford Abbots. Thus, two of the brothers were living a short distance away from each other in Houghton and Hemingford Abbots. By the 1890's two of the younger brothers, Arthur Anderson Fraser and Gilbert Baird Fraser were apparently already living at Holywell, since the Holywell section of the White Cockade club were playing friendly matches against the Hemingford's section. Robert Winchester Fraser, the third son of the Army surgeon, lived intermittently at Hemingford Grey, since only his 1888 entry to the Royal Academy bears that address. His address in the other years up to 1892 was in London or Middlesex.

Robert Winchester Fraser, M.D., died in 1892 and was buried in the churchyard at Hemingford Grey. His wife moved to the Manor House, Fenstanton. Death came again to the Fraser family in 1895, when George Gordon was drowned in the river. One February afternoon, he and his wife went skating on the frozen river. Mrs. Fraser went home to get ready for tea while George Gordon continued skating. He was never again seen alive. His body was discovered some weeks later in the river. He lies buried in the same grave as his father in Hemingford Grey. His wife, upset by rumours which her husband's disappearance had caused, went to live with her children in the West Country.

In 1894 the Old Manor House in Hemingford Grey was the home of John William Dibdin Heseltine. His daughter, May Heseltine, married Gilbert Baird Fraser in 1897. May Heseltine, incidentally was the great aunt of the Right Honourable Michael Heseltine, M.P. The couple then appear to have settled in Reed Cottage on the Front at Holywell. Shortly afterwards, Garden William Fraser and his wife left "The House in the Fields" and went to live in Holywell, where they eventually took lodgings in the Ferry Boat Inn. Robert James Winchester Fraser, the eldest son of R.W. Fraser and the grandson of the Army Surgeon, was living at Spring Cottage, Holywell, near his uncle Gilbert Baird Fraser. His wife, Sarah Hargreave bore him three children. Of these, the eldest, Francis, took holy orders and became a priest.

Thus, by the beginning of the century, there were no Fraser artists living in the Hemingfords or in Houghton. Four of the artists had settled in Holywell, where they remained for the rest of their lives. Another member of the family whose whereabouts are more difficult

Reed Cottage
Home of G. Baird Fraser

to trace is Francis George Gordon Fraser, the brother of Robert James. There is a suggestion that he lived in Middlesex, but he must have visited Holywell, since he produced innumerable stereotyped river scenes which are still found in the district with labels on them such as "The Ouse at Holywell". Finally, there are two more Fraser artists who may have had some connection with Holywell. One signs his, or more probably her, work "Florrie Fraser". It is not evident who Florence or Florrie was, but the watercolours have a family likeness. Another rather typical Fraser river scene of an unidentified view is signed "F.M.F. '09". It is possible that this is the work of Francis McGreigor Fraser, the first son of Arthur Anderson, who is thought to have been a professional actor, although not a successful one.

Several paintings have been seen which look as if they had been painted by a member of the Fraser family, but which have different signatures. W.D. Storey was a Huntingdon artist and house painter working at the beginning of this century who signed watercolours bearing a strong resemblance to the work of F.G. Fraser. A possible explanation of this is that some of the Frasers held art classes in which they imparted their skills and techniques to others. No doubt such classes contributed to their finances. Presumably, W.D. Storey was a pupil in one of these classes. Other signatures which appear on watercolours which are reminiscent of the Frasers include "F. Vincent", "G. Dice", and "Alex. Gordon". It is reported that Robert James Fraser would sign the work of his students, presumably to make the picture more saleable or to add prestige to it.

Spring Cottage
Home of Robert Winter
(County Record Office)

The signatures of the Fraser artists can be confusing, since many of them share the same family christian names. The Dover artist, Francis Arthur Anderson, signed "F.A.F." or "F.A.F. Fraser". Robert Winchester, the third son of the Army surgeon, signed "R.W.F." or "R.W. Fraser". His son, the Holywell artist, signed "Robert Winter". Garden William signed "W.F. Garden", very often in an inconspicuous position, such as on a river bank in the lower half of the picture. The name "Garden" in some documents is spelt "Gardener". It was also the christian name of his paternal grandmother. Arthur Anderson typically signs with an "A.F." monogram and the date in red watercolour. Gilbert Baird signed either in full or as "G. Baird" or with initials. George Gordon used the signature "G. Gordon Fraser" or with initials on illustrations. "F.G. Fraser" is thought to be the signature of Francis George Gordon Fraser, brother of Robert James. Of course, artists may vary their signatures as the occasion demands. Style and content should be taken into account before making an attribution, rather than relying on the signature alone.

Although the Frasers are well known for their scenes of the river Ouse and its villages, it should be noted that the earlier paintings were not necessarily landscapes of Huntingdonshire or Bedfordshire. George Gordon, for example, painted in Ireland and Scotland. he also produced cartoons and illustrations for magazines such as "Fun". He painted scenes illustrating old fairy stories and folk tales, such as the "Goose Girl". The Thames valley seems to have been popular as a source of river scenes with several of the artists. Similarly, R.W. Fraser painted in Suffolk and Norfolk, which is not surprising since he spent some part of his life living at Worlingham and Mildenhall. So far as is known, the Holywell Frasers painted only in watercolour, possibly because they preferred this medium, but also possibly because of the expense of oils and canvases. None of the brothers appear to have been even moderately well-off. There are many stories of how they would paint a picture to settle a debt. They were by no means the only artists to pay in kind. Some poor quality sketches with a Fraser name may have been painted in public houses for a glass of beer.

The Holywell Frasers do not appear to have exhibited in London. George Gordon and R.W. Fraser appear regularly in the Royal Academy lists between 1876 and 1893, but no artists living at Holywell appear to have had their work accepted in London. Perhaps they were too busy earning their living to bother about exhibiting in London.

Grave of Alistair Hay Fraser and his brother Francis McGreigor Fraser (Motto translated: I am Ready)

Grave of Arthur Anderson Fraser and his wife Margaret

Both in Holywell Churchyard

Also, the type of picture accepted for exhibition changed. In the Royal Academy, at least, there seem to be fewer watercolours of old watermills and similar scenes after the turn of the century than before. The Frasers had to compete with the "modern" movement and inevitably they would have lost some potential customers because of this. Since the local market must have been easily saturated, the brothers took steps to sell their pictures over a wide area. In those days, St. Ives had good rail connections. There are reports of the brothers boarding trains in the morning with bundles of pictures under their arms. They sold these to outlets such as furniture shops in places as far away perhaps, as Colchester or Northampton.

One can imagine that the lives of the artists at Holywell in the years before the Great War were tranquil and joyful. The families were growing up and the artists were at the height of their powers. However, fate was drawing its net around them. Arthur Anderson had died in 1904. Grandmother Fraser had also died at about the same time. R.W. Fraser died in 1906. He had been divorced from his wife for several years, a fact which probably caused him to live away from the others. During the war, Arthur Anderson's second son, Alistair, joined the Royal Flying Corps and died in France on active service three months before the armistice. Garden Fraser died in 1921, reputedly by hitting his head on a stone after falling in the dark

Grave of Gilbert Baird Fraser and his daughter Mary T.H.D. Fraser in Holywell Churchyard

outside the Ferry Boat Inn. Francis, of Dover, died in 1924. Then, in 1930, Francis McGreigor, the eccentric actor, caught pneumonia, apparently while wandering around at night without sufficient clothing. He was nursed by his cousin, Robert James, but died in February. Robert James himself, fell ill of the same disease and died a fortnight later. One can imagine that an old cottage on the edge of the Fens is not a good place to be ill in in the winter. Thus, by 1930 only Gilbert Baird and possibly F.G. Fraser, whose date of death is not known, were still alive and painting. Gilbert Baird lived on, but eventually died in February during the cruel winter of 1947, thus bringing to an end the association of the Fraser artists and Holywell.

Grave of Robert Winchester Fraser and of George Gordon Fraser in Hemingford Grey Churchyard. (Motto 'Je suis prest')

It is said that when Gilbert died, he left a houseful of pictures. Reports said that the house was papered in pictures. At that time, Fraser pictures had little value. In desperation, his wife put the whole lot on the garden bonfire, as there was no other way of disposing of them. Forty years later, the best of the Fraser pictures were selling for four figures in the London salerooms. Fate has a hard way of treating those who paint for a living.

Because the Frasers were established at Holywell for over fifty years, it should not obscure the fact that several other artists, of considerable merit, also lived in or painted in the village. In 1890, Thomas Hodgson Lidell (1860 - 1925) was living at Moynes Hall, He first came to London from Edinburgh and then moved to Holywell, where he stayed for about five years. He then moved to Devon and various other parts of the country. He was a member of the Royal Society of British Artists in 1905 and exhibited widely and frequently around the country. He had, for example, 83 pictures in Walkers Gallery, London. He was a landscape painter in both oils and watercolours. In 1909, he visited China and published a book illustrating his visit. His paintings are not seen often in the locality, but a fine watercolour view of St. Ives from the Hemingford Meadows has been seen, as well as several smaller views.

John W. King and his wife Emilie were living at Holywell in 1908 and had moved to Huntingdon by 1918. They then went to live in Scarborough. John King is described as a figure and domestic painter. Local scenes in oils have been seen as well as several etchings of Cambridge Colleges. He had 45 paintings in public exhibitions between 1893 and 1924. Emilie King was a miniaturist. Mrs. Mary Wilmer (see the chapter on Aunt Mary) cherishes a miniature of herself as a little girl which had been painted by Mrs. King and given to her as a present.

Among the visiting artists, Mary Wilmer also remembers Alexander Ignatius Roche (1861 - 1921). He came to stay with Mrs. Wilmer's parents who let rooms to visitors. His purpose in coming to Holywell was to recover from a serious illness and he was accompanied by his wife and small daughter. A.I. Roche was one of the "Glasgow Boys", a group of painters working in Glasgow at the end of the last century and whose work is now avidly sought after. An oil of Houghton Mill has been seen, although none of Holywell as yet, but no doubt he would have painted in the village. He was a landscape and portrait painter and visited Italy and the United States. For the last part of his life he lived in Edinburgh. Over 200 of his paintings were in public exhibitions.

The Fens held an attraction for Scottish artists and several painted in the area, but not necessarily in Holywell. One who should be mentioned is William Miller Frazer (1864 - 1961). It will be noted that his name is spelt with a "z" and this should distinguish him from the artists of Holywell. An oil by him of a misty summer's view of St. Ives Bridge is in a local private collection. This chapter is largely based on a note entitled "The Frasers: A Local Family of Artists". This was written by William Andrew baird Grove for the first comprehensive exhibition of Fraser family paintings which was held at No. 4, The Quay, St. Ives, Cambs, May 5th to June 1st 1980. Another source of information is the article by Charles Lane in Country Life, June 28th 1979, entitled "Art as a family Affair: The Fraser Brothers".

C 1 *A River Landscape, by Bradford Rudge*

C2 *The Fraser Brothers at Camp, by George Gordon Fraser*

C 3 *All Saints Church, St. Ives, by W.F. Garden*

C 4 *Manor Farm and Holywell Parish Church, by Arthur Anderson Fraser*

Hemingford Abbots, by Gilbert Baird Fraser

C 6

Berry House, Holywell, c1900, by Robert Winter

C 7 *Landscape, by Francis Gordon Fraser*

Chapter 4

For King and Country

You went to the verge, you say, and come back safely?
Some have not been so fortunate - some have fallen.

Conrad Aiken

The Parish memorial to those who gave their lives in both the first and second World Wars is in the form of a Portland stone obelisk at the juncture of High Street and Overcote Lane, Needingworth. it was unveiled in December 1920 and paid for by public subscription. Nearby, close to the village lock-up with the date 1838 above the iron grilled door, is a glass encased Roll of Honour on which are listed all the names of those from Holywell and Needingworth who served in both wars. There are 94 names on the first roll, and 48 on the second.

War Memorial, near the Lock-up, Needingworth
(County Record Office)

The men in whose memory the memorial was erected are:-

1914 - 1918

Harvey Attwood
Harry Charles Cooper
Harold James Dodson
Frederick Easton
Alistair Hay Fraser
Harold Ernest P. Gaunt
Cyril Prior Gaunt
Henry Charles W. Hoskyns
Joseph Mansfield
Fred Metcalfe
Ernest Seekings
Herbert Seekings
William Martin Turner
William Walton
Sydney Wilmer

1939 - 1945

Pte. William Freeman
Pte. George J.A. Lantaff
Lieut. Kenneth S. Mills
Sgt. Cyril A. White
Pte. Terence Rayner

The names of Harry Cooper, Henry Hoskyns, and George Lantaff are not on the memorial. Harry Cooper and George Lantaff are memorialised on the Cross of Sacrifices at St. Ives, and Henry Hoskyns in Holy Trinity Church at Folkestone. In the Church at Holywell the memorial altar has the names of the dead of both World Wars inscribed on its panels, including all fifteen from the first and five from the second World War. This memorial was consecrated by the Bishop of Ely in September 1922.The brass altar cross and candlesticks were presented by Mrs. Elizabeth Fraser in memory of her son, Alistair. Close by, amongst the graves of his family, is a memorial stone to Alistair Fraser, bearing the family crest of a Stag's head and the motto 'I am ready'. William Martin Turner, whose grave is near the west boundary of Holywell church-yard, is the only one of those who fell in the Great War to be buried in England.

The Cross of Sacrifice
St. Ives

AT THE GOING DOWN OF THE SUN

AND IN THE MORNING

WE WILL REMEMBER THEM

"For a high cause he fought and fighting died,
Paying with cheerful heart the soldier's price.
Here is no cross of tears, only our pride,
Hath raised this witness to his sacrifice."
(This poem is inscribed on a soldier's grave in France)

Chapter 5

Fishermen and Wildfowlers

Learned of every bird its language, Learned their names and all their secrets
Talked with them whene'er he met them.

'Hiawatha.' Longfellow.

The name of Metcalfe is inextricably linked with the history of Holywell. No other family has continuously lived in the village for so many generations. For centuries they have followed the occupation of fishermen and wildfowlers, and passed from generation to generation a love and knowledge of fenlore, of the river, and its environs.

Dorothy 'Dolly' Arnold née Metcalfe, Tom Metcalfe Arnold's mother

Tom Metcalfe-Arnold whose distant grandsire in 1750 mortgaged the family home 'Wildcroft' for the sum of £10 (Tom holds the actual document) will on his death bring to an end centuries of village craft and tradition. The national census of 1841 shows that Metcalfes then not only lived at Wildcroft, but were also at both the Ferry Boat Inn and at the Pike and Eel, Overcote Ferry. Tom's grandfather was a professional punt gunner. His gun weighed 17lbs had a two inch bore and fired over a pound of shot. By moonlight on a winter evening, perhaps in flood conditions, the boat with it's gun mounted would be silently paddled by Tom lying on his stomach in the stern toward the night resting place of a flock of duck or wigeon, when 70 or 80 yards away the birds, ever watchful, and becoming aware of approaching danger, would take off in whirring flight from the water, then with judgement of the moment the gun would be fired and a crashing boom echo across the waters as a dozen or more birds fell to the shot.

Today's Tom has followed in his father's footsteps and also been a punt gunner. Both have held a well deserved reputation as fen

Tom Metcalfe 's punt gun, weight 107 lb, 2 inch bore. Fires 1 lb of shot.

sportsmen. Old Tom taught scores of Cambridge undergraduates the art of fowling with gun and dog. A good gun and a good dog are essential to a wildfowler.

Fishing the river Ouse was also part of their livelihood, and a day's fishing with Tom as mentor was much sought after. I recall his showing me how maggots were 'farmed', a smelly business, and then sold in old tobacco tins to fishermen out for a day's sport on the river.

The Metcalfe's have always made their own design of eel trap, fashioned from locally grown osiers - these are baited and submerged to the bottom of selected spots of the river, and once the eel is in the trap there is no escape. The fens have always been known for an abundance of eel, and it is not unusual for individuals to weigh 3 or 4 pounds and be 36 inch in length. If lucky enough not to be caught they may well be 30 years of age before the urge to reproduce calls them back to the Sargasso Sea.

The tale is told of Great Grandfather Metcalfe setting off for London with a watercart full of live eels. The horse stopped on the way for a drink at a roadside stream. As it raised it's head from the water and jerked the cart back on the road, the wheel came off and the water cart

Laying an eel trap

crashed on to the road, the eels shot out in a wriggling cascade and the whole lot escaped into the stream.

A seasonal occupation is rush gathering and marketing. Like to many occupations it is deceptively simple and calls for the skill and knowledge of a lifetime if success is to be achieved. The bulrush - Scarpus Lacustris - is a tall upright plant with a smooth green almost leafless stem. It grows best in shallow clear running water, and there are a number of places both up and downstream of Holywell where it has becomes established. In July or August according to the season, the rushes are gathered using a long handled rush hook, loaded on to flat bottomed punts, and transported to the ripening area on the green in front of Tom's house. Here they are carefully dried, avoiding mould if too wet, and brittleness if too dry, sorted and bound into sheafs ready for despatch. Eventually being used for chair seats, rush mats, and various other crafts. They were used to caulk wooden beer barrels in the old days before the advent of the metal barrel.

To most of us the plant which displays brown sausage shaped flower heads, and is common in roadside ditches and damp places is known as the bulrush, but that plant is the reedmace and not a bulrush at all. The misconception came about by the error of a Victorian artist. When

Cutting the rush harvest

painting the picture of 'Moses in the bulrushes' from the biblical story, he in fact showed the cradle hidden in a clump of reedmaces - which were more spectacular to paint than the bulrush.

As I chatted with Tom, the scene from his sitting room window was one which generations of Metcalfes have grown up with, but never taken for granted, and countless artists have striven to capture with their paints. A setting sun reflecting a mackerel sky (not long wet, not long dry) in the water, as the river idly lapped at an old punt moored to a tree trunk stranded from a winter flood. Across the brook golden kingcups nodded beneath the wispy green of springtime willows. A scene constantly changing as night falls, and a swan effortlessly rides the downstream current, to the call of a moorhen.

Smoke from Tom's pipe rises and drifts across the fading rays of the evening sun and a raised glass of amber liquid catches the reflections. Head on paw, the old dog murmurs from dreamland and drifts back to retrieving the wild duck. That is Holywell! Two hundred and forty years on from the day that an early Old Tom took out his £10 mortgage. Taken all in all, it was not a bad investment.

A family of swans

Chapter 6

The Ferryboat Inn; The ghost of Juliet Tewsley

There is evidence that early Stone Age settlers made their habitation in the vicinity of the river crossing at Holywell, and certainly by the time of the Roman occupation there would have been a ferry of some sort to transport goods from one river bank to the other. What better place than this to build an Inn? This Inn or Ale House as it probably was, would have been constructed of daub and wattle, in a similar way to the early Church which was known to be well established by the year 969 a.d. There are blackened beams of old bog oak in the present Inn which dates from the 14th or 15th century, and these solid timbers may well have formed part of a much earlier construction. One likes to think that Gode the Priest sent here from the Benedictine Convent at Ramsey in the year 990 a.d. enjoyed a drink of ale as he chatted with travellers resting on their journey. That the Inn was established before the Norman Conquest, which as every schoolboy knows, took place in 1066 a.d. adds credence to the claim that The Ferry Boat is the oldest Inn in England. Until the river Ouse was controlled by the sluice gates at Denver it was tidal, and the waters rose to the steps of the Inn. It was in these early times that a beacon was mounted on Church Hill to guide craft across the fens to safe harbour. More recently jetties were constructed near the Ferry Boat for the unloading of coal and other merchandise.

Nowadays, the river is busy with pleasure cruisers, whereas before the coming of the railways and well constructed roads most of the river traffic was commercial. Much of the merchandise to the Fairs at St. Ives was transported by river craft. The people of Holywell made good advantage of this by brewing large quantities of ale, and you may be sure the Ferry Boat was a busy place at such times. By tradition the ferry was owned by the Innkeeper, so it would have been prudent of the regular traveller to partake of minehosts hospitality.

In the first National Census of 1841, 10 men gave their occupation as brickmaker, and one as a tilemake; with wives and children they accounted for 27 of the village population which then totalled 192. Two of the single men lodged at the Ferry Boat. The brick kiln was situated behind the Inn, and here too was a row of dwellings occupied by

W.F.Garden *The Ferryboat Inn* *Sothebys*

lightermen and traders. All of these have now disappeared, the clay pit has been infilled and levelled off to form a large car park for patrons of the Inn. The Inn itself has been modernised in recent years and has excellent facilities for the 20th century traveller.

The ferry existed into the 1930's and Sid Tabbitt recalls seeing sheep being driven from the Fen Drayton drove on the drawbridge for passage to pasture on the Holywell side of the river, and that on reaching the halfway point the animals were made to swim the remainder of the crossing for cleansing of their fleece. The drawbridge was swept away in the swirling waters of a severe flood in the 1930's and never replaced.

St. Patricks Day, March 17th, is an important day in the calendar of the Ferry Boat Inn. By tradition it was on St. Patrick's Day in the year 1050 that Juliet Tewsley committed suicide after being spurned by the boy she loved. It is said that on this day, each year, her ghost rises from the grave and walks toward the place of her tragic death. Watch has been kept each year on the anniversary sometimes to midnight and beyond, and many claims have been made of a ghostly presence. Recently a couple who were strangers in the district called at the Inn and ordered some drinks at the bar, whereupon, the lady said she had to leave. When her husband asked her why she wanted to go, she told him the place was haunted. They left the Inn and did not return!

It is a sad story, and there is more to it than just folklore. Juliet Tewsley was a pretty village maiden and she fell in love with a wood-cutter, one Thomas Zoul also of Holywell. One day as she was wandering through the woods picking wild spring flowers she caught a glimpse of Tom as he passed on his way to work. The next morning keeping vigil, Juliet waited until Tom approached then stepping in his path, offered him a bunch of flowers freshly picked. But broad shouldered Tom who preferred nine pins and ale to girls, pushed Juliet aside and told her to go home to her mother. This love of Juliet's was no calf-love. Humiliated and white faced, but with steady step she made her way to the outhouse behind her cottage home and picked up a hemp rope. Then she walked slowly toward the trees near the river, and there from the branch of a willow tree she hanged herself - to bring to an end her unrequited love.

W.F. Garden, Over Church, seen from Holywell

Because she had hanged herself she could not be buried in the sanctified ground of the churchyard, and she was buried near the place of her death by the crossroads, and the grave marked by only a simple slab of grey granite; (the significance of the 'cross' will not be lost upon the reader). This stone is incorporated in the floor of the bar at the Inn, where it has been beyond living memory and supposedly marks the spot where Juliet's mortal remains were buried.

It is from this spot that Juliet's ghost is said to rise on St. Patricks day. A few trees are all that remains of the woods in which Juliet played; the river in which she swam glides peacefully by on a summer afternoon; willow trees sway gracefully in the breeze, and the slab of granite is there for all to see. As for Juliet; each year on St. Patrick's Day she and her true love are remembered.

Chapter 7

The Pike and Eel Inn, Overcote

The Pike and Eel Inn, Overcote Ferry
(County Record Office)

A pleasant walk of about one mile eastward of the Ferry Boat Inn along the floodbank is the Pike and Eel Inn. The raised bank follows the old course of the river. In the 14th century the river changed it's course somewhat to the south, thus adding several acres to the Parish. This is the area of The Lakes, and one field is still known as 'Poor Man's Lot'. The Inn now much enlarged and modernised dates from the 17th century. The area is now known as Overcote, whereas the early house which occupied the site was Over Court. The ferry which no longer exists connected Needingworth in Hunts with Over in Cambs.

My grandfather, who lived in Cambridge for a time and had family interest in Warboys frequently used the drawbridge when travelling to and fro' in his pony and trap. By so doing the journey was reduced by several miles. In flood conditions the crossing could be quite frightening, and my grandmother, of somewhat nervous disposition, would sometimes refuse to accompany him unless he agreed to take the road via St. Ives, or Earith. In more recent times I recall ringing a bell from the Over side of the river, and being taken in a punt with my bicycle to the Needingworth side for a charge of six pence.

Oliver Cromwell is reputed to have planned some of his campaigns at Over Court, for the house once belonged to Colonel Hampden (his cousin). A "secret" stair by a 15th century stone fireplace formed an easy method of escape should the necessity for a quick departure arise.

One Monday morning in 1908 as Mr. F. Metcalfe was going down the river near Over Cote Ferry with his dog he had a shot at a wild duck. The dog crossed over to fetch it, when a large otter tackled the dog, and after a very sharp tussle on land, it dragged the dog into the river where they still fought till they got into midstream. There they both disappeared. the body of the dog was soon afterwards got out and buried at Over Cote. The Hunts Post newspaper dated 24th October 1908 reported that "the river between St. Ives and Over Staunch is getting overrun with otters which destroy a large number of very fine fish every season".

The Pike and Eel Inn, Overcote Ferry
(County Record Office)

Chapter 8

"Aunt Mary"

This life's mostly froth and bubble,
Two things stand like stone:
Kindness in another's trouble
Courage in your own.

On the 25th June 1892 in the early hours of a mid-summer morning, the young occupants of No. 1 Manor Farm Cottages, Holywell, were awakened by the cry of a new born babe, as Amelia Tabbitt gave birth to her ninth child. The new arrival, destined to be the last of Amelia's children, joined four sisters and four brothers who with their father Frederick Tabbitt occupied the tiny cottage. Amelia's maiden name was Cooper and Fred had fetched her from the village of Yelling to be his bride, and with the years, mother to his now large family.

Fred and Amelia Tabbitt
with their daughter, Mary

Through hard work and a keen interest in livestock he had risen to become Head Herdsman to the Sanders Spencer herd of Large and Middle White Yorkshire Pigs at Manor Farm. Mr. Spencer was later to acknowledge that Fred Tabbitt's remarkable knowledge of the breeding and showing of pigs had made a significant contribution to the success of the herd. In the course of his work he had travelled the countries of Europe and accompanied prize winning pigs at all the major agricultural shows in Victorian England.

Although there was overcrowding, by today's standards, in this tiny two up and two down home, with it's candles and wood burning fires - there was no shortage of love. Amelia had ample for each and every one of her growing family. There was discipline and order - there needed to be in a home where there were insufficient chairs, or space, for all to sit at table, and meals were often taken on the stairs by the older children. And so this new arrival was christened Mary by the Rev Hosykins in the Parish Church of St. John The Baptist, and grew up to become a graceful and charming young woman.

In time the family moved to Berry House along Holywell front where Fred kept a small herd of five cows, and horses 'Jenny' and 'Fisher'. They grazed the paddock, and the grass verges of the village road. Fred would sometimes take a sick person in his pony and cart to the Doctor at St. Ives, or collect medicines from the surgery. Amelia Tabbitt was proud of her family and they must have made a brave sight as they made their way to Church on Sunday. Mary was 'confirmed' and for all her long life only illness would keep her away from her spiritual 'well'.

Holywell had become a centre for artists, and one of these fell in love with, and would have taken Mary for his wife, but she chose to stay with her family in their village home, until the day that Walter Wilmer proposed and they became man and wife (Walter's sister married Mary's brother David). They lived in that beautiful old house 'The Pantiles' which had been acquired by Dr. Robinson, a London Surgeon, as a country home from which he could pursue his leisure interest in the sport of fishing. Walter was largely responsible for laying out the garden of the Pantiles as it is seen today, and Mary was Housekeeper to the family.

Mary had long looked on Briar Cottage, next door to the Pantiles, as her 'dream home' and when it came up for sale she urged Walter to buy it. 'No' said Walter 'We cannot afford it on my wages as a Gardener'. However, Mary was not so easily put off, and on the day of the sale she set off for the Corn Exchange, St. Ives, where the auction was to take place, in some trepidation but nevertheless determined. On arriving home later on in the day Walter's greeting 'Well! How much did it make' was met by Mary's excited reply 'It made £120 and we've bought it'. It was something they never regretted, and Mary's dream became their home, to be enjoyed for many years until the sad day that Walter died on 31st May 1971, and was laid to rest in the shadow of the Church they both loved.

Briar Cottage, 'Aunt Mary's' dream home
Built in 1654 and rebuilt in 1988

Mary was to live on in Briar Cottage for many years, alone but not 'lonely' for she is by nature optimistic and cheerful. Typical of the English Country Lady for years she was a familiar sight as she made her way about the village on her 'sit up and beg' bicycle wearing her 'Miss Marple' hat. Loved by generations of children and grown-ups, however busy she may have been, she was always ready to jump off her cycle with a cheery greeting and sympathetic ear.

Now in her 99th year, 'Aunt Mary' Holywell's grand old lady, a resident at 'Rheola' St. Ives, is ever ready with her welcoming smile and the same sparkle in her eye. In a thank you letter to an old friend, for a bunch of springtime Holywell King-cups she wrote:-

Make new friends but keep the old,
The new are Silver,
The Old are Gold.

It is a good philosophy for life.

Chapter 9

Moynes Hall

If thou has a woe, Tell it not to a weakling.
Tell it to thy saddle-bow, and ride forth singing.

(Saying of Alfred the Great)

Moynes Hall is the oldest substantial house in the village, and is the last house on the north side of Back Lane. It is now the farmhouse home of Mr and Mrs Owen Morton who can trace it's history back to the Domesday Survey of 1086. In the survey reference is made to nine

The White Horse public house, Back Lane, Holywell (County Record office)

hides in Holywell held by Ramsey Abbey. One of these hides was held by Aluuold, who it would seem was the fore-runner to one of the owners of Moynes Hall, for the holding of Berenger Le Moyne in Holywell was in 1252 assessed as one hide (a measure of land enough to support a family, perhaps 120 acres). Berenger Le Moyne was a knight, a military tenant annexed to Ramsey Abbey. Old records show that it was bought with Barnwell St. Andrew, County Northants, under the name of Needingworth by Abbot William de Godmanchester on behalf of the Abbey in 1276.

Moynes Hall was later acquired from Thomas, Son of Alexander East, Gentleman, by William Chaderton in 1580, Rector of Holywell 1570 - 1579 and President of Queens College, Cambridge. He it was who built the present house as it dates from the 16th century.

There is part of a moat remaining and three fish ponds. There are, also, three old posts incorporated into the walls of a former cartshed which appears to be posts of an aisled hall. In the 1920's the Butcher family lived here. Old Johnny Butcher had no fingers to his right hand - they had been bitten off by a fractious horse! He became confined to a wheelchair and was much given to the constant and defiant repetition of a swear word in common use at that time.

Moynes Hall, Holywell

During the First World War Mr. Butcher bred heavy horses for the Army, and the tale goes that on one occasion he received a duplicate payment for a consignment of horses. Being an honest man he informed the procuring agent of this, and was informed that it was impossible for the 'Army' to make such a mistake, so he kept the cheque and with it bought some cows which formed the nucleus of the herd which was to replace horse trading when the war ended.

The Butchers' eventually sold Moynes Hall to Mr. Egbert Athelstone Jennings, a gentleman memorable to me because I was once threatened with a good hiding from his 'bullock whopper'. The Orchard at Moynes Hall is separated from Back Lane by a very substantial brick wall. This wall was probably built in the 18th or early 19th century with 'seconds' from the kilns of the nearby brick and tile works.

In this orchard and clearly visible from the road was a large apple tree, always laden in the autumn with shining bright red fruit. Although we had an extensive orchard at home, the occasion arose when these apples were to prove to be too great a temptation, and overcoming all my better instincts I one day succeeded in climbing this wall and dropped down on the other side. The grass beneath the tree was strewn with apples - a 'bitter' disappointment, they were quite uneatable and I was later told that they were cider apples. Looking to return over the wall I then found that the inside was in much better condition than the outside and quite impossible to climb. With grazed knees and sore arms I made my way to a distant gate, and it was then that I was confronted by the waving 'bullock whopper'. There was no escape and the verbal chastisement was to form part of my early education.

Chapter 10

A Wartime Incident

Per Ardua Ad Astra
(The Royal Air Force Motto)

One evening in the summer of 1943, the Second World War was at it's height and I was returning to my R.A.F. Unit after a short leave when I met by chance, on number six platform of Cambridge Railway Station, an old friend, Tom Arnold of Holywell. Tom looking resplendent in his Sergeant Navigator's uniform was returning to his Squadron at Royal Air Force Tuddenham, near Mildenhall. The squadron was in the process of being refitted with Lancaster bombers. We exchanged our wartime experiences during the course of which Tom told me the following tale. Compared with our big cities Holywell had a peaceful war, no bombs were dropped on it's inhabitants, although searchlights probed in the sky to the night-time drone of enemy bombers on their way to the midland towns. The glow of London burning had lit the southern sky. Houses had shaken as a bombladen aircraft exploded on take-off from Warboys airstrip but, by and large, there was nothing to mar the every-day peaceful sounds of village life. Until one summer afternoon for a few moments there was noise and excitement for one resident leading to her sudden downfall.

Tom Arnold's grandfather at the White Horse Public House

To return to Tom and his story...' It was a beautifully clear afternoon and we were returning to base after a trip to R.A.F. Benson in Oxfordshire where cameras had been fitted to our aircraft. We were roughly following the course of the river Ouse when I suggested to my skipper that we take a look at my home village of Holywell, as our course would take us almost overhead. He agreed, and passing over St. Ives we reduced height and followed the line of Meadow Lane to Holywell. Now with Holywell being some 22 feet above sea level (did you know you could travel to Moscow without touching any higher ground?) the Skipper was suddenly confronted with a rise in terrain that he had not expected. He pulled back on the 'stick' and with engines roaring, we just cleared or maybe clipped the elm trees on Church Hill. I had a clear view of the village as it passed beneath us and there was Beatty Carter, Licensee of the White Horse public house looking skyward as she came into the back-yard of the pub with a crate of bottles in her arms. Enjoying my first airborne look at Holywell, the incident passed from my mind.

The next time I came home on leave I called in at the Ferry Boat as was my custom you know, and was greeted by 'Hey Tom, what about this - last week one of your lot came over low and Beatty Carter hearing engines roaring hurried out to look, fell down the pump hole, broke her ankle, and a crate full of beer. She's a bit upset with the R.A.F., so I should give the White Horse a wide berth if I were you'. Of course, said Tom 'I didn't let on - it wouldn't have done would it!'

Tom Arnold, back row, fifth from left

Chapter 11

The Windmill

North of the village on the East side of Mill Way stood the manorial windmill, first mentioned in the year 1279, and again when it was the subject of a dispute between the Abbot of Ramsey and his tenants in 1385. The last mill to stand on this spot was a post mill with a brick and tiled round house at it's base, for the convenient storage of grain and flour. A friendly miller would, given a good wind and a slack time, grind, without charge, the small quantities of grain gathered by gleaning the harvest fields by the poorer families of the village. The mill used to be luffed by a tail pole. One pair of sails had canvas and the other shutters. The body of the mill had two floors with two pairs of stones. Peak and Burr on the second floor. The main post was 21 inches through and was fourteen sided. The earliest inscription was "A.W. 1741" (probably Arthur Watts). The mill was last used by Mr Senescall of Needingworth to grind cattle feed - he was once struck by lightning while rolling up the sail canvas during a thunderstorm.

Holywell post mill, circa 1929
Huntingdon Record Office

By the 1930's the mill had fallen into disuse and it was the intention of the owner Mr. Fred Harvey of Needingworth to dismantle it for safety reasons. However, he sold it to Mr. Tom Paisley of Holywell Manor who had similar intentions, but over the years the structure dilapidated and the mainpost stood gaunt to the sky. In the shadow of the mill stood the miller's cottage, a low picturesque yet sorry looking dwelling occupied by the Papworth family. One night in the early 1940's the family were asleep in their beds when a storm arose and what remained of the old mill came tumbling down. The grinding stones, still to be seen leaning against the cart shed wall by the road at Manor Farm, Holywell, landed against the wall of the bedroom where Joan Papworth, teenage daughter of the family lay sound asleep and unaware of the nearness of the fallen stones. On being wakened and told, she became petrified at the thought of her narrow escape and danger to her life had the stones or mill post crashed through the ancient roof or wall of the cottage. For several minutes she could neither speak or move, to the great alarm of her mother. Eventually, the cottage was considered unfit for human habitation and it too has since been demolished.

The Watts family were millers in Huntingdonshire for generations owning and operating both post and tower mills. Thomas Watts (1822-1903) inherited from his father the brick built tower mill at Hemingford Grey, built in 1820. There had been a mill on this site since the 13th Century and the new mill was built on the mound of the post mill which it replaced. Thomas built or bought a post mill for each of four sons. One of these was the lovely named Black Eagle Windmill, situated behind Eagle Lodge at the top of Houghton Hill. It is shown on the O/S map of 1902 but had disappeared by 1924. One of the sons did not appreciate his fathers benevolence, and had a reputation for gaming and drinking. He was said to spend more time with his friends beneath the mill than attending to his business up above. This must have been a great trial to his father - the family were dissenters and worshipped at the Union Chapel, Houghton.

Erastus Watts,
the last Huntingdonshire windmiller

My Uncle, Erastus Watts (1853-1933) inherited the Hemingford Mill from his father Thomas Watts and was grinding corn on the day of his death 23rd January 1933 - the mill had the distinction of being the last working windmill in Huntingdonshire. I spent many happy hours with him, and on one occasion Beauty and I took a cartload of oats to be ground for cattle feed - there was a fair wind - which I expect prompted my father to send us - and we brought it back ready for use that same day. A well maintained mill needed only a fair wind - gales were a great worry and many mills became runaways. After my Uncle's death my aunt and I frequently climbed to the top of the mill and with wooden mallet checked that the braking chocks were in good and tight. A frightening experience in a gale, one had to shout to be heard against the creaking and groaning of the timbers, flapping of the sail boards, and motion of the cupola against the wind. I think it must have been the nearest thing to life aboard one of Drake's battleships.

Thomas Watts had a frightening experience when he narrowly escaped drowning during a skating expedition. I have a yellowed newspaper cutting dated 1896 in which the author (unnamed) speaking of the pleasure he obtained from skating continued - 'One severe winter I went up to Huntingdon one afternoon, not all the way by the river, but by the brook opposite 'Ashby's Meadow'. On coming back about 4 o'clock crawling under the bridge we heard cries of distress from someone where we knew there was a large hole, which had been open all through the three months' frost. I exclaimed to my friend 'There is someone in that hole'. We skated to the place as quickly as possible, and arriving there found Thomas Watts, the grinder in Houghton Mill, in the hole, his legs drawn by the stream under the ice, and our motion caused the water to splash into his mouth. We had to take our straps out of our skates, strap them together, fasten a stick to one end of the strap, and throw it to him. This took some time, as our straps were frozen in the holes of our skate-boards. Watts in the meantime kept saying 'Make haste. I cannot hold out much longer'.

'We soon rescued him, and he told us that he had seen the last persons who were skating backwards and forwards go home for the night, he not having succeeded in making them hear his cries for help, and had quite given himself up for lost up to the time we appeared on the scene.' He is alive now, lives at the top of Houghton Hill, and works the windmill situated between Hemingford Grey and Victoria Terrace 1896.

In 1932 Ogdens, the Tobacco Company featured on card no 19 of their cigarette card series 'By the Roadside', the tower mill at Hemingford Grey.

Chapter 12

Holywell Manor

The Manor House, Holywell, before restoration
(County Record Office)

The present Manor house dates from the 18th century, and has since changed hands a number of times. It was much altered and modernised by Mr. C.J. Churton after the first world war. There is a well beneath the scullery floor which is reputed to be of ancient origin, and is sunk into the same strata of gravel as that of the spring from which the village takes it's name. Until the arrival of piped water it supplied the household and dairy needs and was never known to run dry. The temperature of the water was such that the glass of a tumbler would cloud over with condensation on receiving water direct from the well. A small petrol motor pumped the water directly into a large tank placed in the roof space of the house. On those occasions when the motor was needed to drive an elevator or other farm machinery a hand pump was brought into use - a laborious task lasting until the overflow pipe signalled that the tank was full.

The Manor House after restoration

It is conjectured that there was a Romano-British settlement on the site of the farm. Roman pottery sherds have been found, and the paddock at the rear of the house is known as the Vineyard.

On Thursday, July 15th, 1888, at about 12.15 during a shower of rain, a flash of lightning was instantaneously followed by a deafening peal of thunder, to the great alarm of the villagers. At this time a large and partly decayed Lombardy poplar, which stood in front of the Manor House, and but a few yards from the front door, was struck and shattered into pieces, while some 70 panes of glass in the windows of the house were broken, and the debris strewed the lawn in front of the house - indeed it presented the appearance of the effect of an explosion of dynamite. Upon visiting the farmyard close by soon afterwards Mr. Spencer found that a corner of a barn had been struck, and the door of a closed pig-sty partly splintered. A sow within the barn, which was suckling seven young pigs, was killed instantly, but the young pigs were unhurt. The house was again struck by lightning on 25th May, 1889.

As a child I was warned never to shelter during a thunderstorm beneath the trees in Conger Lane, because the ash trees there were frequently struck by lightning, and I recall one old tree being struck and set alight. Electrically charged storm clouds coming across the flat fens would on reaching higher ground have the right situation for a discharge of electrical forces.

St. Oswald Apiary, Holywell: Mrs F. Richardson

Mrs. Sanders Spencer, wife of the famous breeder of pigs, had a keen interest in bee-keeping. She established an apiary in the Manor grounds, and in honour of St. Oswald who purchased the Manorial Rights from King Edgar in the 10th century, named it "St. Oswald's Apiary". She was a well known exhibitor at local shows and won many awards. In one season, after a hard winter, her ten hives, all bar framed, produced 550lbs of honey - a considerable achievement.

Chapter 13

Middle White Pig

To eat, drink, sleep.
What then?
To eat, drink and sleep again.

The Holywell herd of Large and Middle White Yorkshire Pigs was established by Mr. Sanders Spencer at Holywell Manor in 1875. He had been interested in the breeding of pigs since 1862 and on taking up residence at Holywell quickly built up the herd by purchasing the best pigs available, not counting the cost, having for his object the improvement of his stock. He did not always buy from the best exhibitor, but frequently made forays into the northern counties inspecting the stock of some of the oldest breeders of pigs who were not exhibitors at shows, and who therefore did not spoil their stock by fattening them up, but kept them only for breeding purposes.

Large White Boar — 'Holywell Czech 2nd'
First and Reserve champion at the Royal Show, Lincoln, 1907
Owner: Mr. C. Spencer
(by permission of Mr. & Mrs. G. Johnson)

He could often see the parent and sometimes the grand-parents of those he bought so that he could be tolerably sure of the style of pig that he could expect as a result of crossing them with his own best pigs. When the offspring did not turn out as well as he expected he would clear out the whole of that line, knowing full well that no herd of animals is so quickly spoilt as a herd of pigs.

He was particularly interested in the Middle White pig, and was almost solely responsible for the development of this breed. The line started as a cross between two other breeds. One was the Large White which had been evolved as a backyard pig in the early nineteenth century by weavers and other factory workers in the West Riding of Yorkshire, the other was the Small White which was introduced into England in the eighteenth century via eastern Asia and China. The new breed suited the Victorian taste for juicy succulent pork, from an easily managed quick growing pig.

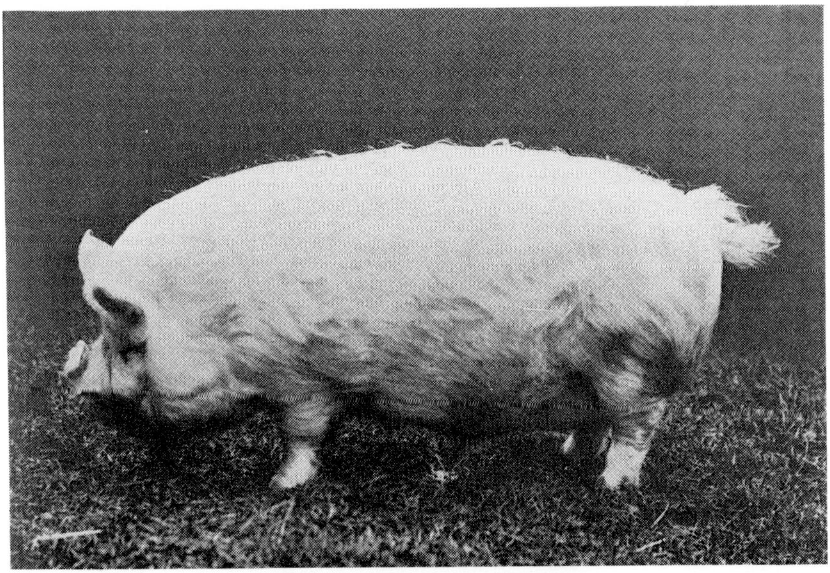

Small White Boar 'Walton Pippin'
Owner: Mr. C. Spencer

Shortly after his arrival at Holywell he was urged by his friends to exhibit some of his pigs, but he put it off until 1877, then sending a few to the County Show he was surprised by his success and the result was an attack of "Show Fever". The following year he exhibited in three classes at the Royal Agricultural Society's Show and obtained the first prize in two, and the second in another. One of the successful pigs was

"Pride of Oxford", a sow, she was never beaten, and won 11 first prizes, and 2 champion prizes.

After that he had so much success in the following years that the demand for his pigs became so great that he was compelled to increase his herd and increase his piggeries. During 1881 his pigs won as many prizes as those of anyone else. In time he found it almost impossible to shown to any extent and keep up his stock to the high standard upon which he was determined. The demand for Holywell pigs greatly increased both at home and abroad, and Holywell became something of a mecca for pig breeders from all over the world. His customers found that the pigs had been naturally fed, not forced, and that they invariably turned out well, producing stock equal to themselves. Sanders Spencer then concentrated on saving his best pigs for breeding purposes, instead of spoiling a great many of them in fattening them up for shows - the custom at that time.

He became Honorary Secretary of the Pig Breeders Association, in much demand to lecture, and to write for the agricultural press. He wrote the complete section on the 'Management and Feeding of Pigs' for the Livestock of the Farm Encyclopaedia.

Of his beloved Middle White he says 'It is doubtful whether any pig is bred to such perfection of form as the Middle White...the sows are excellent mothers, gentle with their young, and permitting the

Middle White Boar 'Holywell Rosador'

attendant to handle them almost at will, even so far as to examine their teeth...they fat with great freedom, are soon ready for the butcher and cut up remarkably well.'

During the six years that he regularly exhibited at the major shows he achieved 204 first, 118 second, 2 third, and 26 Champion Prizes. Many Gold Medals and prize money of more than £1500. In one six week period he shipped 124 boars and sows, mostly to old customers. Of these one went to France, two to Rio de Janiero, 21 to Austria, 22 to Germany, 24 to Holland, and 54 to Switzerland where they were established as the breeding stock for the Swiss Agricultural Society.

By the year 1908 the herd had passed from father to son. Mr. Spencer having 'The Croft' built at Holywell for his 'retirement'.

Mr. Charles Spencer also had considerable success in the show ring. In the year 1907 he won first prize for large white boars at the R.A.S.E. Show at Lincoln. First and Champion at the Royal Counties show, First at Yorkshire, thus winning first prize for Boars under one year old, under two years old, and in the aged boar class.

First prize was also won for the best Bacon Liveweight under 220 lbs at the Suffolk Show. The herd continued to grow and prosper until on 15th July 1913 when Mr. Charles Spencer left Holywell to take up residence at Brampton where the premises were inadequate for a large herd and the Holywell herd was dispersed at auction apart from a few old sows as a nucleus of a future herd.

Eventually, eating habits changed and the fat succulent pork of the Middle White, became replaced by the long lean pig of the Danish Landrace breed. Today the Middle White is a rare breed kept only by a few enthusiasts.

Holywell was also well known in the show ring for the herd of Dairy Shorthorn Cattle but these had a subordinate position to the White Pigs. Extensive records were kept of both the shorthorn and pig herds..

It is perhaps unique to Holywell that the 1871 census gives the occupation of both father, Samuel Rufell (61) and his son, Samuel (29) as Castrator, which is an indication of the size that the Holywell herd of pigs attained.

The herd received innumerable testimonials expressing satisfaction of which the following is a small selection:-

Canada 1887: They are the best pigs in Canada.

Russia: Pigs arrived safe in Russia and give complete satisfaction.

Home Farm, Sandringham: The two yelts arrived safely and very good ones they are.

Chadwell Heath: I am pleased with the boar but think him a little dear.

Dorset: I like the young boar at home even better than at Holywell.

France: The boar is greatly admired by our farmers and peasants, all pig raisers, one and all are anxious for his services.

Felhampton Court: The young sow is the admiration of all her beholders.

Derby: I went to the Royal to try and buy another yelt off you, but you had gone home. I was persuaded to buy off another breeder but have regretted it ever since.

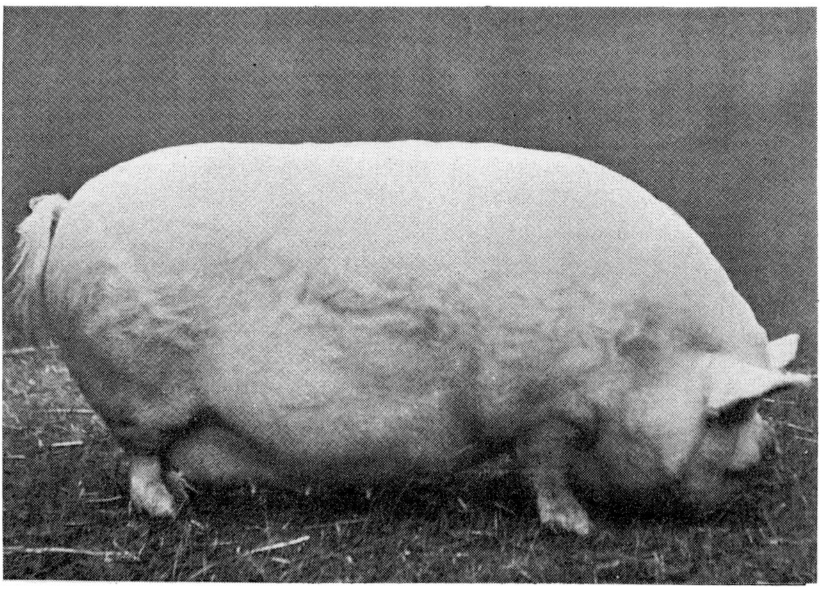

Middle White Sow 'Holywell Perfection'
Owner, Mr. C. Spencer

In all, the herd won 2500 prizes and exported to 45 countries. Many large whites went to Denmark for breeding purposes and their genes must still be in the pigs which provide bacon for our breakfast table today.

Mr. Sanders Spencer lived at Holywell for 55 years and only left the village the year before his death in 1931 in his 91st year. He had the distinction of being permitted to use on his stationery the Royal Arms and the Prince of Wales' Plume.

At the herd dispersal sale all the best large white pigs were bought by Mr. J. Chivers of Histon where they continued to flourish and won many more prizes at the most prestigious shows in the country.

Chapter 14

The White Cockade Club

"Prone merum et tales. Pereat qui crastina curat"

In 1745 Prince Charles Edward Stuart, 'Bonnie Prince Charlie', landed in Scotland from France in an attempt to win the British Crown for James his father. After some initial success by the Highlanders the British Army finally routed the Scots at the battle of Culloden on 16th April 1746, and any serious threat by the Jacobites to the Protestant throne had ended. Even so, one cannot doubt the sincerity of the romantically-minded Fraser family, domiciled in the Huntingdonshire villages of the Hemingfords and Holywell, far from their roots in the Highlands of Scotland, in their support of the Jacobite cause however lost it may have been.

Together with friends they founded the 'White Cockade Jacobite Club' with it's headquarters, naturally enough, at the Ferry Boat Inn. Founded in 1890, the club expanded with branches in Wales, Ireland, Scotland, Northern England, the Thames Valley, London, Brighton, France and Spain. The Club held frequent convivial evening meetings at the Ferry Boat for like-minded people, and although these sometimes degenerated into the singing of bawdy songs they were for the most part peaceful gatherings.

A regular toast proposed at these gatherings was 'To the little gentleman in Black Velvet - the Mole'. The Scottish Jacobites had a great dislike amounting to hatred for the Dutch Protestant King William of Orange who, with Mary, had replaced the Catholic King James II on the throne in 1689. William met his death in 1702 from an injury sustained when thrown from his horse - the horse had caught it's foot in a mole run and stumbled!

The activities of the club did occasionally hit the headlines of both the local and national press. In 1895 a very important event took place when the prospective Parliamentary Jacobites' candidate for North Huntingdonshire, Herbert Vivian addressed the annual meeting. He said 'the Government has no right to send a policeman round and shut up the public houses at ten o'clock at night'. (applause !). He also wished to see the overthrow of the Royal Family of Queen Victoria, and to see 'A Merrie England and a happy England once more' - he did not get elected.

'Oak Apple Day is the 29th of May', and commemorates the restoration to the throne of Charles II in 1660; Nine years earlier, defeated at the battle of Worcester, his hiding place for six weeks was a hunting lodge in Shropshire, where during the day Charles hid in a hollow oak in the grounds. In celebration of this event the Holywell Jacobites held an annual quoits match at the Ferry Boat Inn. The Holywell team usually won, having the advantage of regular practise. In the evening 150 or more Jacobites and friends gathered in the Inn for a 'smoking concert' to sing Jacobite songs and hear speeches, the ladies being excluded on these occasions. A.A. Fraser was President (and referee of the quoits matches) G.G. Fraser, was Chairman, and G.B. Fraser, Secretary - also playing the fiddle to accompany the songs.

The London Daily News, June 1890, reported that 'The Jacobite White Cockade Club got up last Oak Apple Day a remarkable demonstration by challenging the Royal Oak Jacobite Club of Hemingford Grey to a friendly quoit match as the best means of commemorating the day. The notion of restoring the Stuart Dynasty by the agency of a friendly quoit match is ingenious and probably their own. The Holywell men began preparations by hoisting boughs of oaks on to the tower of the Church. These they lashed to the weather-cock and pinnacles amid much applause, which was intensified when similar items were discerned on the summit of Swavesey Church across the fen. The main street and the Ferry Boat were adorned in like manner. The next day came the

Oliver Cromwell's statue in the Market Place, St. Ives

Hemingford men, some one hundred and twenty strong, and after the quoit match there was a great rejoicing at the old riverside Inn where every Jacobite deposited an oak spray on the long table before seats were taken and toasts went round and Jacobite ditties sung'.

The 'Fiery Cross' of January 1902, the magazine of the Scottish Nationalists advocating the Restoration of the Royal Stuart Family to the throne, referring to the unveiling on 23rd October 1901 of the statue at St. Ives in memory of Oliver Cromwell was glad to note that 'the Jacobites in the neighbourhood did not allow the humiliating spectacle to proceed without protest'.

The Peterborough Standard stated that something akin to consternation went round the great assembly at St. Ives during the proceedings, when it was reported that the statue had to be watched at night in fear of a plot of the Jacobites - whose headquarters are in the area - to blow it up. This was followed by the intelligence that 'material' had been seized. 'Material' in the popular mind being dynamite.

So there was a ferment. Enquiry at the police station tended to allay the alarm, for it was found that the material confiscated was a collection of ropes, halters, and nooses, labelled for various prominent people. The Jacobites it was said, had hired two men to throw these into the crowd during the speech making, and incite a row. Under these circumstances the police went to a public house in the town and bagged the lot. A sample of these offerings were:-

> *'To the detestable memory of a blasphemous hypocritical murderer' from A. Anderson Fraser.*
>
> *'In memoriam Oliver Cromwell. Cheated the hangman September 3rd, 1658' from Gilbert Baird Fraser.*

On being interviewed both gentlemen said they had nothing to conceal, but on the other hand they were going to take Councel's opinion with a view to prosecuting the police for illegal seizure of their property.

> *'But the police seized them in the interest of law and order - what mad-headed idea was yours to throw them into the crowd?'*
> *'That was not our idea' was the ready reply. 'We desired to have these placed with the wreaths at the foot of the statue. Was there anything wrong in that? Our opinion of Cromwell is as legitimate as that of those who put the*

wreaths there surely?'.
'Throw among the crowd: Pshaw!, We are not hooligans! We are men of peace - but men of opinions, and opinions we don't intend to conceal' said G.B. Fraser.

Dr. Ranking, in a speech shortly before the unveiling said '..I find myself among men who hold Jacobite principles not as a mere sentiment, however beautiful and romantic, but as a Faith, and who by that Faith govern and regulate their lives.

The authorities chose to take no action in the matter. On the 30th January 1905, a wreath was placed along with others beside the statue of King Charles I in London. 'From the White Cockade Legitimate Club, Holywell, Hunts. To the Memory of the illustrious King Charles beheaded by his rebel subjects on 30th January 1649.' with the words -

'Cursed be the heart that had the heart to do it,
Cursed be the blood that let this blood from hence'

Charles I's statue in Whitehall

The statue to King Charles I was cast in bronze by Hubert Le Sueur a Huguenot sculptor in 1633 for Lord Treasurer Weston. During the Commonwealth it was sold to a brazier named John Rivett for melting down, but although Rivett sold many objects supposedly made from the statue, he had in fact with foresight buried it for safety. After the restoration of the monarchy it was purchased by the crown and erected at the top of Whitehall looking toward the site of the execution.

A few years ago I was in Trafalgar Square on the 30th January when my attention was drawn to a lone figure in highland dress standing at the foot of the statue and playing a lament on the pipes. A bunch of red roses had been placed on the plinth representing the spilled blood of 'Charles the Martyr' and nearby were several bunches of snowdrops reminiscent of tears. The Frasers would have liked that!

Tragedies within the Fraser family began a decline in the activities of the 'White Cockade Club', and eventually the coming of war saw it's demise apart from an occasional nostalgic gathering. But the Frasers continued to hold strongly to their belief in the Jacobite cause. As a boy attending school at the home of G.B. Fraser I can verify that Oak Apple Day was not allowed to pass without anticipation and recognition. There was a build up over several days of stories, especially of Scotland's history. The Highland Clans, Robert Bruce, Bonnie Prince Charlie and his escape to the continent by the aid of Flora Macdonald etc. Sprays of oak leaves were gathered from the tree which yet stands by the Manor gateway and taken to join others already at the school. On the big day and arrival at school a spray of oak leaves was ceremoniously pinned to each jacket or dress. A spray of leaves was placed over the porch and at various places about the room. There were no lessons on that day, but more stories of scottish heroes, and games in the garden - and lemonade to drink.

Although exciting enough for us children, it must have been an annual trip down memory lane for the Frasers.

'Set down the wine and the dice
and perish the thought of tomorrow'.

Chapter 15

Where folk live well and long...

Where folk live well and long... is the headline of an article published in the *Hunts Post* newspaper of September 1924, illustrating the large proportion of elderly people living in the twin villages of Holywell and Needingworth at that time. It concludes that life in these villages was happy as well as long.

A number of octogenarians were named as living in Holywell. Sanders Spencer (84), Mrs. Mortlock (84) George Cooper (82) and another aged resident who wished to be spared the publicity.

A long and healthy life was attributed to the clear spring water filtering through the purifying gravel bed of the region and to the clean fresh air coming directly from the north sea across the open fen land. The water now arrives by pipe and tap, and the air is not quite as pure as it once was, so there must be some other ingredient to account for the longevity of the present residents of both villages. Research into the subject resulted in a hesitant claim on behalf of hard work, supplemented by a wink in the telling, and a more positive and thoughtful attribution to a 'contented mind'.

Mary Wilmer, equally well known as Mary Tabbitt (at Holywell, girls retain their maiden name long into their married life) is now well into her 99th year, while Jarvis Victor Carter is enjoying the 104th year of his long life.

I listened, with something akin to awe, to Vic's story. He was born in the days of hand reaping with the flail still in common use, at a time when almost all the agricultural work on the land was accomplished by hand tools with the horse pulling cart and plough.

Vic recalls the excitement brought about by the Boer War and the burning of the town pump on St. Ives Market Hill during the Relief of Mafeking celebrations; the coming of the motor car and the aeroplane, radio and television through to the present age of computers and travel by jet aircraft. His memory of the First World War is "as vivid as if it were yesterday".

Born on 11th June 1887 in one of a pair of cottages in the living of the Rector, he was forecasted to be born a girl and named Victoria in honour of the Queen. But nature carried on regardless, and at birth the baby was seen clearly to be of the opposite sex so the name was shortened to Victor, preceded by Jarvis out of respect for his Uncle Bill who lived at the Ferry Boat. His father was coachman/groom at the rectory for The Rev. Hoskyns. Uncle Bill, operated the ferry across the Ouse and charged a penny for each passenger making the crossing by boat, and sixpence for cattle and each wheeled vehicle using the drawbridge. Holywell ferry, like that at Overcote, provided a short cut in journeys to villages beyond the river and to Cambridge in particular. Mr. Carter would sometimes take the rector's girls by brougham via the ferry to dancing and May Balls at the Colleges in Cambridge.

There he would wait, often until two or three o'clock in the morning, before returning via the ferry again to Holywell, and still be expected to ring the servants rising bell at 6 a.m.

At eight years of age Vic became a member of the church choir. He had a natural aptitude for music and singing and, recognising this, his father took him each week by pony cart to St. Ives where he took music lessons at the home of Mr. Tyrell in East Street. Later, he studied the organ with tuition by Mr. Halton of Earith, at that time organist at St. Ives Parish Church. At the age of nineteen, he was officially appointed organist at Holywell by The Rev. Norgate. This was the beginning of a lifetimes love for the instrument and of service to the Church at Holywell, Fenstanton, Bluntisham, Wilburton, and Somersham. Eventually, back again at Holywell, his doctor forbade him, because of his age, to drive his motor car and for eleven more years he was chauffeured by his friend Doris Stokes of Pidley. Vic now has a two manual electronic organ beside his chair on which he occasionally plays a tune but finds it "not the same as a real pipe organ".

His childhood home was next door-but-one to that of Mary Tabbitt and he well recalls her as a young girl delivering milk in a can for her father to the village homes. Beatrice 'Beatty' Carter at the White Horse public house, was his sister. At that time John Day the carpenter and his sister, kept the Anchor Inn. A baker named Godfrey of Needingworth delivered bread to the village and he would frequently neglect his round for the delights of the Inn.

Godfrey's pony was normally patient enough quietly grazing the grass verges by the roadside, but one day he wandered toward the brook until the cart toppled in taking the pony with it. Godfrey came out of the Inn to find the upset, and his bread floating down-stream toward the river. An incident recounted to the down of many a cheerful pint at the pub - lit by candlelight and paraffin, with a log fire, and rushes on the floor. A home brew was served to the pervading scent of plug tobacco

Chris Bedford, Postmaster and Grocer at Needingworth, made a weekly round of the village delivering the previous weeks' order and listing requirements for the following week - at the same time he delivered 'the pension' to the elderly folk.

The outbreak of war in 1914 saw Vic working at Fullers coach-building works in New Road, St. Ives, later to be burned to the ground in one of the fiercest fires seen in the town. Next in the road was Fowell's Engineering Works and here, working at the lathe, was Gilbert Baird Fraser, a near neighbour of Vic's and by persuasion a conscientious objector known to his workmates at 'Gengy', pronounced as in 'Genghis Khan'.

Vic answered the call to arms in 1915 and volunteered for the Hunts Cyclists, going first to Filey, in Yorkshire for training, where he was quickly spotted as a marksman with the rifle. In due course this led to his becoming a sniper when drafted to France. The tone of his voice lowered and he hesitated as he recalled memories of those terrible days - "I've seen men standing up in the mud - dead! I've turned to speak to a comrade as he fell by my side - shot!".

By 1917 his battalion had been joined to the Warwicks - "I'll have your breeches one of these days Carter" said the Sergeant, for such was the humour of the front line where life could be very short for the unlucky. (The Hunts Cyclists wore breeches and leather leggings, whereas, the Warwicks wore K.D. and puttees).

Vic became a runner, carrying word-of-mouth messages from the front line to Company Headquarters. Word of mouth only, in case of capture by the enemy in the maze of trenches mud and barbed wire. He came to know the battle area so well that he led replacements up the line and brought back battle weary troops for a respite.

At Passchendaele he "went over the top" by the side of the company commander Lieutenant. Crighton of Wales, who was killed and at the same time Vic fell, wounded in the thigh. He lay as if dead and watched as a German soldier robbed Crighton of his "lovely watch" and other equipment. He lay there until the morning when during a lull in the fighting a man from Godmanchester crawled up. "What's up Carter?" he said, when told he bound up the leg. Then Foggy Beeby from Yaxley carried him back to the Field Dressing Station to begin a painful journey back to Blighty, Trent Bridge Military Hospital, and eventual return to civilian life. "And" said Vic with a smile, "the Sergeant nearly got my breeches, but not quite".

Vic as he has always been known, is a Queen's Man, and rightly proud of having fought for good old England. He married a girl from Somersham and settled down to a life in the commercial world, becoming well known to the farmers throughout the county as he supplied their poultry and animal feed requirements. Now widowed, he has for twenty years enjoyed the companionship and care of Rosie Stokes, herself a widow and octogenarian, and the friendship of Maurice her foster son.

The Marriage between Andrew Williams and Sally Rose, of Bluntisham, took place at the Church of St. John the baptist, Holywell on the 19th December 1970. The ceremony was conducted by The Rev Hugh Pettingell. Vic Carter played the organ, and is seen playing the final hymn 'Praise my Soul the King of Heaven'. This event also marked his official retirement as Church organist — seventy-six years on, since he first sat a few feet away from the organ in the choir stalls as a boy chorister.

Peter Dumbleton, of Cambridge, took the photograph.

Part II

A Childhood Remembered
1922 - 1935

To see a world in a grain of sand, and a heaven in a wild flower;

Hold infinity in the palm of your hand, and eternity in an hour.

Blake

Chapter 16

In the Beginning

That is the land of lost Content,
I see it shining plain,
The Happy highways where I went ,
And cannot come again.

A.E. Housman.

I was born in November of the year 1921, in the town of St. Ives; safely into the sure hands of Nurse Briggs, wife of Jack the plumber and signwriter. She had delivered many a child in her long life. Probably no great event to her but for me the beginning of a childhood filled to the brim and overflowing with the joys of a happy home and life on a farm.

My father was an Oxfordshire man, born out of generations of yeoman farmers in the year 1866. He was a working farmer. On winter evenings, sitting in the warmth of a log fire, his thoughts would go back to the hardships of his youth, and occasionally he would talk of those early years. Not with any rancour, for by all accounts they were a happy family - he had five sisters. They lived in a thatched cottage and drew water from the well in the garden. The 1861 census shows the family farm to contain 75 acres of land. A horse was kept for ploughing; a donkey for carting smaller loads, and to take eggs and produce to Bicester market. Apparently the donkey would often refuse to work for the girls - to their aggravation - and to their added annoyance when it would start off without trouble for my father. Unbeknown to his sisters he usually had a piece of crust or some such reward to give to the animal on completion of the task in hand.

My father

He was first sent to work in the fields at the age of seven, not unusual at that time, to scare crows from the ripening corn. A clapper was made from two pieces of thin board, placed either side of a central board shaped to form a handle. At the same time he picked stones for maintenance of the parish road. With the womenfolk he hand-weeded the growing crops. The corn was cut by sickle and tied with straw bands. Later to be thrashed by flails and winnowed by the wind. He showed me how to make a wind-proof 'donkey jacket' from a corn sack using binder twine to keep it in place - like a monks cowl with a long flap at the back to keep out wind and rain. There were various versions of this clothing. Generally speaking the 1870 Education Act was ignored in the country areas, and he did not go regularly to school until his teenage years when evening classes were started for boys and girls who worked on the land.

My paternal grandmother Ann, born on Christmas Day 1840, was younger than her sister Hannah and consequently had to leave home. Rather than 'go into service' she became a Dairy Maid at Rousham Park within 'walking distance' of the family home. The House built in 1635 by Sir Robert Dormer is still in the ownership of the same family, and it is interesting to speculate that the fine herd of rare Longhorn cattle are descendants of those milked by my grandmother. My father saved sixpences and shillings to buy a cow of his own, and with the ups and downs of the passing years he prospered and became a farmer in his own right. It was a hard life, which even today with all it's mechanisation and conveniences, is much the same and not for those who want a Monday to Friday, nine to five lifestyle. There is the compensation of working with nature and to the farmer the words 'work' and 'pleasure' are synonymous.

My paternal grandmother

My mother came from a long line of fen dwellers who tilled the good black earth of Turf Fen by Benwick Meer. In her youth peat was still used as fuel by fen families. The turves were cut with a becket, a kind of spade; they would be stacked and left to dry during the summer, then carted home on a turf barrow which was similar to a wheelbarrow without legs. By a strange twist of fate she and my father came together, and three children were born. The eldest being my brother Henry, then my sister Eileen, and lastly me Josiah, to become known as Joe for short.

My mother

My sister made a premature and unprepared entry into the world, on a springlike day in April 1920 my mother decided to visit relatives living in the village of Warboys and harnessed 'Jet' the black, lively, high stepping pony to the trap - a light two wheeled vehicle, rather than the safe but sure cob used for the milk round. She was an experienced driver and the outward journey was uneventful. Time came to return home and Jet made an eager start, no doubt having thoughts of his comfortable stable and a bite of hay. On approaching the bend in the road at the foot of Church hill he would not be held back, took the corner too fast, over-turned the trap throwing my mother into the ditch.

My sister Eileen, myself and my brother Henry

She was knocked unconscious, sustained both collar bones broken and much bruising. Within hours she gave birth to Eileen one might say thrown into the world several weeks early; a tiny babe dependent on the limitless care and skill of Dr. W.R. Grove and Nurse Briggs. My mother's life hung in the balance, for 18 days she laid in a coma but, to

Early days — my sister Eileen

my good fortune, made a slow but sure recovery. Jet was sold!

My mother having been born into a large Victorian family, mostly girls, was sent off to London at an early age to join an older sister apprenticed to a Millinery Salon. The girls slept in a dormitory above the workroom under the watchful eye of the senior seamstress.

The shop was open each evening until 8 o'clock, and the girls graduated from sewing and trimming to serving in the shop - the almost weekly change in trimmings to individual taste was highly fashionable in late Victorian and Edwardian days. On putting up the shutters and closing the shop, the girls had their evening meal followed by lights out at 10 p.m. On Sunday morning the girls paraded to Church - something of

My maternal family group. My mother is standing in the back row, third from left

a fashion parade for the benefit of would be customers of the Salon. The older girls were allowed freedom on Sunday afternoon and took walks in the park, some even met their future husbands. The younger girls were chaperoned.

One day my mother, having been unfairly admonished, packed her trunk and took the train for home. Leaving the trunk at Huntingdon station she walked home to Warboys: Her father was furious and threatened to send her straight back to London, however, he relented and returned with her the following day. He was astonished to see the cramped conditions in which the girls were living and working, and after a short time a domestic situation was found and mother left the millinery trade for good. Going on the become a Ladies Companion and to my great advantage a very good cook. She loved preparing lunch time picnics for shooting parties and for the beaters. Although there were no shooting parties at Holywell it did not need much of an excuse to have a picnic. These could be by the river, at the seaside, in the hay or harvest field, or even on the lawn on a summer's day - a forerunner to the modern barbeque.

My father on the St. Ivo Dairy Milk float

By 1922 father was farming land both to the north and south of St. Ives, and running the St. Ivo dairy and milk round in the town. In that year Manor Farm, Holywell, came up for sale; It was a mixed arable and dairy farm of some 200 acres consisting of the Manor House, with good buildings and stock yards providing an opportunity to carry out his farming enterprise in one unit. The arable land was rich loam with some gravelly loam, a good high pasture, meadow land in the flood plain lying between the north bank of the river and the village, plus a few acres of swampy land. One of the fields known as Tussocks was heavy clay, nearly always waterlogged and covered in clumps of sedgelike grass, later to become a favourite rootling ground for the pigs.

Having weighed up the pros and cons he decided to go ahead with the purchase and so it was in this environment that I first became aware of my surroundings, and to wonder at my good fortune. He had an experienced team of farm workers at St. Ives, and no doubt his own view on life had some influence with the men because all those who were able to do so continued in his employment and joined wholeheartedly in the new venture.

My father with 'Cornerstone' the Shorthorn bull

These were the men I grew up with, they were part of the day going about their work; each had his own task to perform, and a responsibility to the others, particularly at the early morning six o'clock start. The whole effort at that time was to get the herd of Shorthorn dairy cows into their stalls and commence the milking, carried out by hand, so that the 17 gallon churns could be filled, loaded on to the milk float and away to St. Ives by seven o'clock. This was before the age of bottles and refrigerators. The milk was poured from the churn into a delivery can, and then by half or pint measures in to the housewives' jugs. The whole procedure was repeated at three o'clock in the afternoon, and the milk float on it's way by four o'clock.

These men are part of Holywell's history, for several years they worked the land and left their imprint however small, William 'Bill' Leach, Pigman: Continued to live at St. Ives and travelled each day to Holywell by pony cart. His day started before 5 a.m. by candlelight with the lighting of a stick fire to boil a kettle and make a pot of tea. 'Kim' the little black pony had been put out to graze in the Paddock by Rheola in Cemetery Road on returning home the previous evening. Now he had to be caught, sometimes reluctantly, harnessed up to the cart, and the candle side lantern lit for the journey to Holywell. There was little traffic on the road and Kim needed very little guiding. I guess that Bill enjoyed his first pipe of plug tobacco on the way. Once there, Kim would be given a feed in the stable and later released into the

My mother with 'Kim'

Vineyard paddock until required for light duties, or to take Bill home again when work was done. Bill's first job was to help with the milking, then he could start his own job with the pigs. Perhaps boiling up a copper full of 'swill' to be mixed with meal for the morning feed, seeing to the general welfare of the herd of large white pigs.

In his younger days Bill would walk 7 miles each way to court his wife who lived at Raveley - and this perhaps, after following the plough all day. One day I was with Bill in his garden when he plunged his hand and arm into the soil of what was to become his onion bed. "Why are you doing that" I asked. "To see if the temperature is right for the seeds to germinate" he replied, adding "When the leaves of the elderberry bush are are as big as little mouses' ears, thats the time to sow your seed". He had a family to feed and grew some good crops as proof of his theory.

At dockey time, when working in the field, he would sit back into the hedgerow, or against a haystack out of the wind, and take from his rushplaited dockey bag a clean white linen cloth. This invariably contained a good part of a loaf of bread with a chunk of cheese, or much loved salt pork, held by the thumb in the centre. Using his shutknife, given a quick wipe on corduroy trouser leg, he would deftly cut a morsel of each until just enough was left for the final bite. To my fascination it always ended up just right! Washed down with a bottle of cold tea - the usual thirst quenching drink of the farm labourer - it was a meal fit for a king.

John Coulson. Cowman. Came with his wife, son Wally, daughters Amy and Joan, to live in one of the two tied cottages on the farm. Wally worked with his father. Their forebears had been river people, working the barges which plied their trade up and down the river Ouse. They lived close to the river in Wellington Street, St. Ives near to Doo's boatyard. At Holywell their duties included the general care of the milking herd — a difficult calving could mean an all night vigil. Then there was 'Cornerstone' and 'Old Tom' the shorthorn bulls to be respected and cared for. These were joined as newcomers to the team by Bill Stringer and his son George from Needingworth.

After finishing the day's work in the yards according to season there were a hundred and one jobs to be done. Ploughing, cultivating, hedgecutting, dyking, corn drilling, harrowing, reaping, mowing - the list is almost endless.

George Teat, Horsekeeper: moved into the other tied cottage. his day started really early. Horses could not be sent straight out to the fields. They needed to be fed at least an hour before being called upon to pull the various implements of cultivation. In the old days when hirings were made at the Michaelmas Fair; farms were often known by the number of horses needed to work it - Manor farm was a six horse farm.

When the horses came home after the day's work, usually about 3 o'clock they were brushed and currycombed, fed and watered, then given a period of freedom in the pasture. Horsekeepers took great pride in their charges and in their wellbeing. Each horse is an individual - hence the saying 'you can take a horse to water but you cannot make him drink'. A horse will work his heart out for one man, and yet be really difficult with another. Also, some horses would pair up better than others. To be successful a horsekeeper needed to know all the little foibles of his charges if the best was to be obtained from them. We had a horse named 'Smart' she was young and always keen to work, but she had a sensitive skin and even a fly settling on her back would be enough to set her off, so she had to be carefully handled. One day going back from the rickyard to the harvest field with an empty cart George Reynolds was riding Smart side saddle, as was the usual custom, when she shied at some object and was off! It could have been a nasty accident, but George being acrobatic jumped clear and there was not harm done. However, father said No more riding saddle with Smart it is reins from the cart in future!

After a time George Teat left to take up a post as Gamekeeper nearer his home at Abbots Ripton. His place was taken by Bill Leach's son Alfred.

Dick Reynolds. Milk Roundsman/Gardener: I can barely remember Dick he followed family tradition and joined the Army. In the 1914/18 war his father was a gunner with the Royal Artillery, and had a team of horses with which the guns and ammunition wagons were drawn forward into battle line firing positions. Dick served with the 2nd Battalion Grenadier Guards in the second world war. He was wounded in France, and later gave his life at Louvain in Belgium. He lies in the military cemetry at Lille.

George Reynolds with 'Tommy' the milk round pony

His job was taken at the farm by his younger brother George then 16 years of age. George was a member of the All Saints Church, St. Ives Gymnastic Club under the

Captaincy of Ald. E.G. Holmes, and was himself to become an Instructor at the Club. I envied his ability to twist and turn on the water pipes in the dairy. He fell in love with an married Amy, the elder daughter of John Coulson. George biked to work from St. Ives, and in snowy or icy weather found it quicker to use the cross country droves rather than take the high road. His start to the day was to collect the gleaming pails of frothing milk, in warm weather to pass it through the cooling system, and then through clean muslin in to the churns. Harness up the fast trotting cob 'Tommy' to the milk float and get off not later than 7 a.m. to deliver at St. Ives. With a good pony the journey could be done in 20 minutes. The milk pony was changed fairly frequently - he had to be capable of trotting all the way - the housewife wanted fresh milk for the breakfast table, and it was the same in the afternoon for the tea table. On returning to the farm George would have all the equipment to scrub and scald in readiness for the next milking. He was a keen gardener, and had the large garden and lawns to care for - he grew the best sweet peas I've ever seen.

Walter 'Bolcher' Smith, General Farm Worker: On Monday's Bolcher would be off with his stick to St. Ives Market droving for farmers and cattle dealers. Drovers were always in demand, especially at that time of the year when there was an influx of Irish cattle to be de-railed and placed in holding fields, driven to market, and perhaps back to the the fields, or to one of the surrounding farms. In today's parlance Bolcher worked flexi-time. After a good day at market Bolcher might have some sleeping off to do!

In the days before road and rail transport cattle were driven about the country along well established lanes, or droves; many towns and villages along these routes had a 'Pound', being an enclosure in which a drover could safely leave his flock of sheep or cattle for the night, while he sought lodging at a nearby Inn. Any animal found straying in the Parish would be placed in the Pound, and only released to it's owner on payment of a fee.

There is no trace of a Pound at Holywell although it was a cross-roads for cattle movement. There was a Pound at Needingworth of which nothing now remains except the nearby Pound Hill as one enters the village on the road from St. Ives.

Lastly but by no means least, was an itinerant character known as Nati'. Whether or not this was an abbreviation of native I do not know. He would turn up seemingly from nowhere to cries of 'Old Nati's back', take up residence in the loft over the milk float stable, make fires for his billy can or come to the kitchen door for hot water. I think he had a general aversion to water other than for his billycan. He would snare a few rabbits, tell a few tales, do a bit of work just to show willing, then after a short time he would be off again: disappearing down the lane with an old sack over his shoulder containing all his worldly possessions. To appear again in due season, always sure of a welcome back, from us children anyway.

I went with Bolcher one summer evening across the fields to fill up the water tank for a herd of cattle which he was shepherding for a dealer, and grazing a field off Meadow Lane, St. Ives, when on looking in the open fronted byre, we found old Nati asleep in the manger. Having established that he was still in the land of the living, we left him to his dreams. Now! I wouldn't be surprised if Bolcher too had found that manger a peaceful market day resting place!

These then were the men who tilled the soil, milked the cows, and cut the hay. A willing band and my childhood friends.

On the domestic side Miss Ada Robertson, a Londoner by birth, was engaged as nursemaid to replace Nurse Briggs who quite naturally was unable to leave her home in St. Ives and continue the care of my sister and myself, for by this time I had become an added duty.

Jack Briggs had the ability to imitate bird song, and would enjoy this skill, to the astonishment of young children, by pretending that he had a bird hidden beneath his jacket under the armpit. He would encourage a child to look for the bird, with much flapping of jacket and movement: Of course, it was never found, but children were never sure of the truth.

Jack also had a reputation as a charmer away of warts. When I was about 8 years of age I developed a wart on the back of my right hand. One Monday with my father in the market we met up with Jack and after listening to his tame nightingale he held my hand and lightly rubbed the wart saying 'Oh yes, that will disappear', and so it did quite quickly - I have the scar on my hand to this day.

Ada, who was much loved by us all, never really took to the country. The sight of a mouse would send her into hysterics, but she could laugh at a joke and my father would pull her leg unmercifully. Thursday was Ada's half-day off duty, and if the weather was right clean, and dry underfoot, she would go to visit relatives in Needingworth. Street lighting was unheard of in Holywell and it would oft times be dark when she returned home. This led to two little ditties which were chanted to her aggravation.

Ada fell over the dustbin,
It was a funny sight,
Ada fell over the dustbin,
In the middle of the night.
Ada fell down a rabbit hole,
What did Ada do?
Ada fell down a rabbit hole,
Ada lost her shoe.

After some years, and we children were growing up; Ada took up a similar appointment with a family in St. Ives. She had become one of our family and we were sorry to see her go.

Pat Prime was a jolly rotund figure and could just about suffocate a small boy clutched to her ample bosom in warm embrace, and she had a liking for this sort of welcome. Pat came on Mondays to do the washing, and Rose Mansfield also came from Needingworth to help in the many duties connected with the running of a large farmhouse.

We had Floss a wire haired terrier, who regularly produced a litter of puppies, and between time was responsible for keeping down the rat population. A quick dart, bite, and shake of the head would see another rat thrown to one side and ready for the next. A good place to put up a rat was the oat bin the stable.

I've seen her train a puppy to do likewise, and once a rat was used in a tug of war game between them. Then there was Bob, an Old English Sheepdog, who frequently knocked me over with a joyful bound - but whose long shaggy coat was often wet and muddy from the fields. He and Pat Prime had a similar tendency to kiss ones face in welcome, but his attentions were not always welcome as he had a tendency to slobber. My father enjoyed his company, and would simply laugh and say 'Good Old Bob'.

Later, at the time of my father's death Bob laid on the mat outside the bedroom door and could not be coaxed away. He laid there for three days and was never again his 'old self' wandering about as if lost. I know of another Old English Sheepdog who was disconsolate on the death of his master, and would frequently go to the village Churchyard and lay upon the grave.

The North American Indians have a folktale that a dog journeyed to the edge of the world in the east, and there lit a torch form the rising sun; bringing back fire for the benefit of mankind. For this brave deed he was given a place at man's fireside and has ever since been his best friend. It is a nice story.

Chapter 17

Early Days

There was a time when meadow, grove, and stream,
The earth, and every common sight,
To me did seem,
Apparelled in celestial light,
The glory and the freshness of a dream.

William Wordsworth.

The very early years of my life are a kaleidoscope of disjointed memories; of exploring around the house and farm. My sister Eileen and I played well together. One day - did the sun always shine? – we were sitting in the centre of a fairy ring in the pasture making daisy chains for the little folk, when the cows were turned into the field from the afternoon milking: They were curious and we were terrified. It had been a great adventure to creep through a hole in the privet hedge at the end of the garden but now we could hardly get back quickly enough. I always seemed to be in need of a face lift by means of Ada's hanky softly spat upon - it was something I detested - and would squirm away from as often as possible. We looked under the gooseberry bushes for a little brother or sister. We were chased by the gander when going too close to the geese and fell into the pond. We had plates of cream fresh from the pans in the dairy with soft brown sugar.

Dr. Grove sometimes called when in the village for a check of his 'miracle girl'. We were all expected to be there for inspection. One day my brother ran out of the door rather than be inspected - Doctor chased him round the garden and they both came in panting. Another time when I had some spots, he prescribed a raw egg and a glass of nettle tea to be taken daily. Both were horrible, but I survived and came to no harm.

Wandering round the cowshed, Wally would squirt me with a jet of warm milk straight from the udder of the cow he was milking, cap back to front and head pushed into the soft flank of the animal. All had names, order of precedence and their own stall. The scent of cows breath, fresh drawn milk, linseed cake, warmly saturated straw, and the warmth from their bodies made the cowshed a special place to be. I can recall it now with nostalgia, and so different from today's disinfectant-laden milking machines on wet, sterile, concrete floor.

Alf Leach would put me up on Beauty's broad back, as with Boxer, Blossom, Roger, Smart and Bonny the other working horses, she was taken to the trough to drink. Beauty was an ex Great War Army horse and carried the broad arrow, branded on her buttocks. She became my special friend.

I would be sent off when a neighbouring farmer brought his sow to the boar, or the bull was taken from the pen on the arrival of a heifer — but I could peep through a knothole in the stable door and wonder at the goings on. In these ways the early years passed, and out of play small duties of fetch and carry turned into regular duties and schooldays began.

Chapter 18

Schooldays

...except ye utter by the tongue words easy to be understood, how shall it be known what is spoken? for ye shall speak into the air.

1 Corinthians 14.9

Reed Cottage School, at the right-hand of the picture (Ralph Hopton)

I attended the small private school held at Reed Cottage in the Village. The home of Gilbert Baird Fraser, the youngest member of the artist family, and his wife May. Morning class began at 9 a.m. and on arrival at the side door we knocked, waited until greeted, said 'Good morning teacher' to Mrs Fraser, and took our place round the dining room table. The day started with a bible reading, a prayer, and a children's hymn - my favourite was 'Jesus bids us shine' I especially liked the 'you in your small corner and I in mine' ending of the verse.

Mid-morning we had a cup of milk from the can we had brought with us, and a biscuit. The can of milk was sufficient for the daily need of the house. I cannot recall there ever being more than five pupils. Mrs

Fraser was a very genteel person, always both kind and patient.

In those congenial surroundings I began my education, learned the basic three R's and enough history and geography to whet my appetite for more. The daily reading lessons were most to my liking and I soon became acquainted with Beatrix Potter, Alice, Aesop's Fables and others of the childrens classics. At home I advanced from Tiny Tots to The Wizard. I was growing up!

The Fraser's bedroom doubled as a studio. It had a good bay window in which G.B.'s easel was set up, and here he painted in watercolour the ever changing colour and pattern of the fen sky. He would occasionally join our art class — we would have a little bit of squinting along our pencils to learn perspective, and lots of fun with colour washes.

Often we sat without removing our topcoat; firing was expensive, and mainly used in the kitchen. There Mrs Fraser's sister Miss Heseltine unobtrusively prepared the family lunch. Miss Heseltine was supposed to be neither seen or heard, but when the opportunity arose she would give us a friendly little wave, nod or wink, according to the time taken for the door to the kitchen to open and shut as Mrs. Fraser checked the progress of the meal.

Afternoon school was an option dependent on the weather or other activity at home or the Frasers. Occasionally daughter Helen would be at home. This young lady was considered to be 'highly strung' and such days called for quietness as she practised playing the violin. We were apprehensive of a sudden flare up of temper which would upset the whole household, and did nothing to encourage me in the liking of her chosen instrument. Her mother had long since given up an attempt to improve my grasp of music and the mystery of the metronome, supplemented by pencil tappings on the table. My sister Eileen had both an aptitude and enjoyed music; My father purchased a piano for her to replace the rather old instrument we had at that time. It was made by Witton Witton and Co, of London, in solid English oak and strung on an iron frame - it is as good as ever sixty years on. The oak for this piano came from a tree which grew at, or near, my fathers boyhood home at Upper Arncott, for which he had a great affection. The reason for this affection is open to conjecture, but eventually the tree was felled and being told of it he bought a number of planks vowing that one day they would enclose his mortal remains. However, his love for his daughter Eileen was such that her piano was made from this the 'best oak in all England'. When my father died old Mr. Nicholls, Carpenter, of St. Johns Road in St. Ives made his coffin and it could well be that the remaining boards went into it.

Which reminds me that in nearby East Street, St. Ives, one Edgar Skeels the Carpenter/Joiner/Undertaker had his premises. Many years later I had an occasion to call on Edgar for reasons quite unconnected with his profession. Edgar, probably having cash flow problems at the time, offered to sell me on payment of a deposit a coffin made of English oak. He insisted that I accompany him up the rickety stairs to view this beautifully made object of his craft. I declined to accept on the grounds that it looked a little small for one of my stature. 'If you'll buy it, I'll get you in it' said Edgar. I may well have been having an 'off' day, but even so, Edgar's reply was somewhat optimistic because he has long since been called to join his forefathers.

At the Manor we were one of the few houses in the village to have flush toilets; we also had a gas lighting system run on carbide and maintained daily by George when he returned from the milk round.

At school there was no such luxury and to spend a penny was an adventure in itself, although to be avoided if at all possible as the novelty wore off. The privy was a small wooden hut toward the top of the garden. By comparison to many it was a luxury version, being a two holer, one being slightly smaller and lower than the other - ideal for polite conversation or for planning the day ahead. A candle and box of matches were available for winter emergencies, and placed on a shelf which was shared by a robin who nested there.

As a diversion from more serious lessons we did handicrafts. Little mats made from cane and bound with coloured raffia; Kettle and saucepan holders made from sacking and worn out clothing to be earmarked as Christmas presents; Wool balls made from pulled out old pullovers and destined to hang in perambulators and, most practical of all, newspaper cut into convenient sized squares and held together by a loop of string, later to hang conveniently on a nail in the privy. On another nail hung a sacrosanct string of tissue paper having been carefully saved, from shop-wrapped purchases of fancy bread, for the use of guests. In fine weather a visit to the 'wee hoose' made a welcome diversion from learning, but in winter, of necessity uuugh!

Our daily route from home to school was usually by the footpath along the front of the village, approximately half a mile. Only if the footpath was flooded would we take the less interesting back road. Anyone met along the way would have a cheery greeting for us and perhaps make some enquiry of health, or comment on some particular matter of interest in the village on the day: All part of the bush telegraph system of spreading news and gathering information.

Several times during the winter months and occasionally as late as June the river Ouse would flood after snow or a period of prolonged rain.

Spring Cottage, with the brook in flood (Hubert Coop)

The source of the river Ouse is near Farthinghoe in Buckinghamshire where it rises as a spring and begins it's journey to the sea as a small stream. It then travels through some of the largest hay meadows in the country, through Olney, Bedford, St. Neots and Huntingdon to St. Ives and on to Holywell, through the fens, to the sea. A particularly bad flood would follow the opening of the lockgates to relieve pressure of water upstream in the Bedford area. It was reckoned that the Bedford water would reach Holywell in little over 24 hours and add several feet of water to the already flooded meadows. Farmers would be warned that it was time to remove sheep and cattle to higher ground. The control of the river, and it's outlet to the sea at Denver has been much improved since those days. Overnight the water could rise to the very edge of the footpath, being several feet above the road level. All the meadow land on either side of the river deep in water as far as the eye could see, sometimes frozen inches thick, and scarring the trunks of willow trees as the ice broke and mini ice floes crashed about in the receding water. When the flood subsided we would collect pieces of driftwood left at the water's edge and take armsful home to be dried and used as kindling for the kitchen range. What a backdrop these floods made for the biblical story of Noah, illustrated in spring rain by the arching rainbow of God's promise,.

My first stop on the way to school would be to peep through the boarded fence of the garden on the right hand side of the road, to catch a glimpse of the auburn haired princess lying on her couch on the veranda of the summer house waiting for her prince to come and breathe new life into her fragile form. (It was Kathleen Meggy seeking cure in the fresh air for tuberculosis) Sadly, her prince never came! After many years the summer house slowly fell into decay and was finally swept away by a winter flood. Now only memory rests where she lay.

In a hedge-row by The Croft, home of Sanders Spencer a previous owner of the Manor, grew trees of the wild Myrobalan Plum - mellabellars to village children - their branches arching over the footpath, and in early spring a snowlike mass of tiny white blossom bearing the promise of yet another juicy sweet yield in summer days. There were two varieties, the small red one, with which you could play 'Spit the pip furthest' game, and the larger yellow variety which we would gather in a basket and take to Mrs. Fraser for a pie, with another on the way home for my sister to do likewise. The fruits carpeted the pathway and grassy slope. Next on our journey came the Pillar Box set in the brick wall of 'The Friars'. Important looking 'V.R.' on the door, sometimes a letter to pop in its mouth, and on lucky days postman Grey would be there to 'open the box'. Now the box is on a post and has lost all it's charm - spoiling an innocent pleasure to meet some overall plan of uniformity no doubt. There was another post box in the wall of a cottage in Back Street.

In the crevices of the long brick wall grew the wild Catmint with its lavender flowers and pungent scent when crushed between finger and thumb. Among the topmost crumbling bricks grew ancient wallflowers and snapdragons with their mouths waiting to make silent speech. Then came Pretty Lady Betsy draping in pink profusion the wall to Mrs 'Bobby' Fraser's cottage. Autumn was the time for walnuts dropped in the grass from the tree overhanging the path by Hill Farm, Mr William West's home with the date 1623 on the chimney stack. It needed courage and egging-on to dare a quick dash through the farm gate to the other side of the wall, and perhaps to no purpose. By the pathway stood an ancient lightning-struck poplar in which a child could hide or shelter from a passing storm.

On the roadside verge grew many wildflowers. The tiny blue 'Birds Eye' Speedwell which flowered all year round, but not to be picked for fear that a bird might see and peck out one's own eye. The lovely yellow flowers of the Silver Leaf, and Birdsfoot Trefoil our 'Egg and Bacon' flower; Coltsfoot on sturdy stem by the stone-heaps; Pink Mallow, and nectar to suck from the flower of the white Dead Nettle. Most beautiful of all the roadside flowers and harbinger of spring was the Celandine with it's large bright yellow flower held over a mass of shining green leaves:-

There's a flower that shall be mine
'Tis the little Celandine.

William Wordsworth

Dandelion clocks were there to be blown, and pale blue Peri-winkles to be searched for in their mass of green leaf. Not forgetting the humble daisy and the joy of finding one in rare pink blushing finery. 'She loves me, She loves me not' was often played and sometimes a little cheating was necessary as the last few petals fell.

The girls who wear a daisy chain
Grow up pretty, never plain.

Anon

With all these distractions, and many more, the path to and from school was always interesting, and yet I think the homeward path was best.

Chapter 19

My Education Continues

As the weeks followed day by day, so my schooling continued. I well recall being ill with some childish complaint or other, and that Mrs Fraser came in in the afternoons and read to me from The Pickwick Papers which we were at the time 'doing' at school. I believe she enjoyed reading aloud as much as I enjoyed listening, and I'm sure laughing at the adventures of Mr Pickwick and his friends did me as much good as medicine. I did not then look upon it as anything extraordinary that my teacher should call and read, and stay for afternoon tea, but looking back I realise I was a most fortunate boy.

In the fullness of time I reached my eighth birthday and by the following spring was judged old enough to join my brother at the St. Ives Grammar School; motto *Ora et Labora.* The Headmaster was Captain Fraser; retired from service in India. No relation of the Holywell Frasers, and before whom we lined up each morning, with regimental precision, for inspection.

My brother became the proud owner of a new bicycle, and I inherited his old one, wooden blocks being bolted to the pedals so that my legs could reach them. We cycled together on the first morning of term, whereupon I disgraced myself on reaching school by misjudging the kerb and falling off the machine - needing some patching up before parade - wooden blocks on pedals are not easy to control! Introductions over, we afterwards made our separate way to school, and my more formal education began.

Most of the boys were from farming families in the surrounding villages, or sons of tradesmen and shopkeepers in the town. There were three Houses. Cromwell - after Oliver, Dunton - after the poet who at one time lived in the town, and Anderson - because there were nearly enough of them for a house of their own. I was placed in the latter simply to make up the number. Farm boys were allowed home at 3.15 p.m. unless they wished to stay for sporting activities. In the summer whole days off were allowed when needed, to help with work on the farm, particularly at haytime or harvest. I was not built for sport - my feet having been shaped by generations of sons of the soil, and more adaptable to following the plough. So it was with great effort that at the Annual Sports I held the record for coming last in the compulsory 100 yard sprint year by year; I never attempted a longer

St. Ives Grammar School, Henry, front row, second from left.

distance. I also held the record for never clearing a hurdle unless lowered several inches as an Irish handicap to the other competitors.

I had considerable success at arm wrestling. As a farm boy my arm muscles were used to such activities as pitching sheaves, loading muck carts, or wielding an axe, but arm wrestling was then looked upon as a boys' past-time, whereas now it has laid down rules and is likely to be included in the next Olympic Games.

My usual position at football was behind the goal - where I probably had more kicks at the ball than I would have done had I been chosen to play on the field. At cricket I played at the longstop position - to collect up any balls missed by both the batsman and the wicket keeper. You may know that after a certain number of balls are thrown the fielding team changes over and the bowler throws the ball from the opposite end. Some players simply walk the length of the pitch, or step a few paces to the side, but the longstop has to make a circuitous walk to the opposite end of the field. The other players being impatient to get on with the game make a start, and often the longstop will not have long arrived at his new position before it is time to reverse the procedure. The town boys were keen on this game, but I never did find much merit in the whole procedure and only indulged in it if no excuse could be found for going home to the farm.

It is little wonder that my name never appeared on the Victor Ludorum Cup awarded on Sports Day to the best all round athlete.

Mother and I, taken by an itinerant street photographer in St. Ives.

I did excel in the playground game of marbles, and my stock of them proved useful in barter to further my hobby of collecting cigarette cards. I would give other boys a ride on my bicycle cross-bar to the playing field on my way home, or on Mondays to the cattle market which was always an attraction. Most of my cards came from the men on the farm; I was always willing to fetch a packet of cigarettes from the White Horse P.H. for having the card, and sometimes would be teased and sent to fetch a packet of five Woodbines - these were in paper packets and had no cards.

On my way home from school I would jump off my bike to inspect a discarded cigarette packet, and occasionally play the 'trap' game of filling an empty packet with stones, a worm, or some such object and then place it in position for another unsuspecting collector to find. I recall being unable to complete my set of Players History of Naval Dress for want of card No.25. I had searched, and offered all kinds of bribes without success; When on one Saturday morning driving some young bullocks from Holywell to pasture in Lowndes Drove I espied a soggy dirty packet in the roadside ditch - it contained an equally soggy card No. 25. I knew then just how one of my mothers relations must have felt when he found gold in Australia. I suppose the bullocks reached their pasture but I have no recollection of it.

My brother was more interested in the animals and wildlife of the farm, whereas my interest lay mainly with the flowers and plant life. He did not mind getting blood on his hands, but I was a bit finicky especially when it came to dissecting small creatures in the interest of curiosity. At certain times of the year when the moles are active he became expert at catching them; their pelts were deftly removed, spread out and nailed to dry in the wind. Then together with rabbit skins, both tame and wild; Hare and the occasional fox, they would be taken to St. Ives and sold to Mr. Walter Scott for the fur trade.

This was a good source of pocket money for the country boy, but not for me!. The smell of Scott's rag-and-bone department was beyond description, and I would sell my occasional rabbit skin to my brother for half the going rate.

Without noticing any change I became more involved in the daily life of the farm. The first job on arriving home from school was to collect up the eggs from the hen houses, and scatter a bowl full of corn for the laying birds to supplement their free range feeding in the Vineyard, a paddock of some five acres, which they shared with the ponies. A pair of carrion crows made their nest yearly in the very top most branches of an old willow tree that had not been pollarded and this pair was always on the look out for a free meal. They and the sparrow hawk would sometimes snatch a baby chick if it strayed too far from the hen, and particularly from those hens which nested in the hedgerows.

In the spring, broody hens were set in a row of closely confined nesting boxes to hatch out the eggs of selected hens, ducks and geese. They were allowed 20 minutes to eat, drink, and stretch their legs before being returned to another 24 hour stint on the nest. After a day or two they were no trouble and would often return long before the 20 minutes were up. The incubation period for a hen's egg is 21 days and an extra week for the duck and goose. Hatching days, with the miracle of new life, were always exciting. One family of our geese always constructed a nest in the cart hovel beyond the pond, and a great heap of straw, bits of twig, or string from a walk about in the stackyard, took several days and much nodding of heads before the pair was satisfied with the arrangement. Mother goose then laid between 9 and 12 eggs and proudly sat upon them. The gander either stood or sat alongside the nest and woe betide anyone who went nearer than the open front of the hovel. It was a treat to see the family on the pond or on their way to the brook as they became older.

Ducks are quite stupid birds and will not lay in a nest, that is until they feel the urge to reproduce and they will then pluck out their breast feathers, which I suppose is very noble of them and cover the eggs with more 'duck down' each day until they have enough to incubate. Usually, they just drop their eggs whereever they happen to stand at the time of need, and if they have complete freedom that means in the pond. Consequently, the last job at night was to shut the ducks up, not always easy because they had no wish to leave the pond and had to be gently encouraged by movement of a chain drawn across the water and attached at one end to the far side of the pond. In the morning one searched in the none too pleasant straw of the duck-house for their eggs - ours were a lovely blue green in colour, that is, after some attention at the scullery sink. No farmyard is complete without a flock of these garrulous comedians, standing on their head in the pond, or sliding about on it's frozen surface with incredulous gabble, then waddling off with heads dobbing this way and that as they search for grain around the corn stacks.

To hear the excitement in their voices as they greet the new dawn at the water's edge as if nature had provided it overnight for the first time is both humbling and amusing. Maybe they are not so stupid after all, and have innate knowledge that each day is for living as if the first and last.

Chapter 20

Of Birds and Nesting

Free from the cottage corner, see how wild,
The village- boy along the pasture hies,
With every smell, and sound, and sight be guil'd,
That round the prospect meets his wondering eyes;
Now, stooping, eager for the cowslip peeps,
As though he'd get them all, - now, tired of these,
Across the flaggy brook he eager leaps,
For some new flower his happy rapture sees,
Now, leering 'mid the bushes on his knees,
On woodland banks, for blue-bell flowers he creeps,
And now, while looking up among the trees,
He spies a nest, and down he throws his flowers,
And up he climbs with new-fed ecstasies;
The happiest object in the summer hours.

'The Village Boy', John Clare

He that hurts robin and wren,
Will never prosper, boy or man.

Country saying

Most village boys had their collection of birds eggs. Mine were carefully laid out on sawdust in an old christmas cracker box. We did not do any great harm, always left two or three eggs in the nest so that it would not be forsaken, and the bird soon made up the number to the usual clutch. Three seems to be the maximum number of a bird brain mathematical skill. Members of the tit family lay the largest number of eggs and are more easily disturbed than most. We never touched the lovely nest of the Long Tailed Tit, egg shaped with just a tiny entrance hole in the moss. The Robin too was left in peace for fear of ill luck. Had she not on that Christmas Eve long ago, fanned with her wings the warmth of the fire to bring comfort to the Christ child, and been scorched in the doing of it. Her red breast to be for ever a sign of thankfulness!

Almost all birds return year after year to the same vicinity to rear their young - having spent such care in choosing a site, why change it? Blackbirds return to the same old broken fence, or crutch of the yew tree. Starlings returned to the hole in the trunk of an elm tree by the pig sties - often being so keen to lay that they dropped an egg outside the nest. In this same elm nested a pair of Wood Pigeon to wake us early with their repeated call of 'Tak two coos, tak two'. They laid two eggs on a flimsy construction of twigs, and were public enemy number one in the garden, where they were partial to emerging green peas and brassicas. Little Jenny Wren chose the ivy-covered crumbling brick by the kitchen garden wall - here lived the little spiders which made a tasty snack.

The Mavis Thrush nested out of reach in the spread out branches of the pine trees by the tennis court. The Hedge Sparrow laid her bright blue eggs in a nest safe in the branches of the golden privet bush - how nice they looked against the gold - But no! The Cuckoo had been watching and waiting all along, when five eggs were laid and the sparrow ready to incubate them, she stealthily replaced them with two of her own. The nest could offer accommodation for only one cuckoo chick, and we would watch it as it grew to fill the tiny nest - helping out the busy sparrow by popping a caterpillar or worm into the ever open noisy beak of the fledgeling.

House Martins nested under the eaves of the house - Ada said that swallows helped God create the arch of the sky! Swallows nested on the rafters in the cowshed, diving in and out as if not they, but man and beast were the interlopers.

It was said to be 'bad luck' not to have swallows nesting in the cowshed. As with most country superstitions this contained more than a grain of truth - swallows feed on flies, and flies carry mastitis, a disease which causes inflammation of the glands which produce milk. A pair of Wagtails were always busy in the cow yards and they too nested where a brick had become dislodged by the hay-rack.

Three breeds of owl lived on the farm. The white faced Barn Owl who sat in wisdom high up in the grain store, and paid his rent in cigar shaped casts of the undigested remains of rats and mice. The Little Owl was always first to start the evening fly-past, and lived in the Church Tower close by the stackyard wall. In the hollow trunk of a laid over willow tree, on the bank of a dyke in Noble's field there lived a pair of Tawny Owls, one of which played a trick on me. On passing the tree whatever the time of year it was my habit to whack it with a stick to the annoyance of it's inhabitants who would dash out sleepy eyed and screeching, for they would have been up late searching for little voles and unsuspecting birds - they were not my friends! Now, this dyke was known descriptively as the Stinking Dyke, it carried the sewage effluent of St. Ives on a meandering course of a mile or more until it discharged into the river it had a scent all of it's own. This dyke was man-made and formed the parish boundary between Holywell and St. Ives; It was a most un-neighbourly act by the St. Ivians to use the parish boundary for this unsavoury purpose. However, I had on an earlier evening climbed the trunk of this tree and by peering head down seen five round eggs in the nest some four feet down the hole, so this time I had come prepared with a dessert spoon firmly strung to a stick and with the intention of adding a Tawny Owl egg to my collection. The tree was whacked good and hard with no result, so after a further whack I concluded that the owls had set out early for their nightly patrol of hedgerow and bank, and set about climbing the trunk. All went well, and clinging to a branch I twisted and peered into the hole as I had many times before. When with a whoosh and angry screech the tawny owl launched itself talons forward at my face. Instinctively I let go of the branch to protect my face, slipped, and dived head first into the stinking dyke. I crawled out spitting and spluttering soaked in the indescribable filth, made for a nearby hedgerow and washed my head in the cattle drinking trough, and near to tears made my way home, in some fear and trepidation of the forthcoming chastisement which must surely follow. As it turned out, my Guardian Angel came once more to my rescue and my father, who had decided to spend a few minutes spudding up thistles in the pasture, saw his son running haltingly across the fields.

He thought it a huge joke, roared with laughter, and smoothed my homecoming with a strip clean up under the pump before calling my mother. 'You had better go back and find the spoon' he said, but I never did, and I never did get a Tawny Owl egg. Many years later during a Home Guard Exercise a well known St. Ivian fell in the same dyke. One of our heifers almost drowned in the dyke and the more she struggled the more she sank in the soft sludge of the bottom. Good old Beauty was brought and pulled her out by a rope tightened round the heifers horns. She was none the worse after a good swill down with buckets of water and the yard broom. A bucket of warm bran mash, usually reserved for cows in labour completed the cure.

None of our cows were polled, a common practice today when it is as rare to see a horned cow as it was then to see one that by nature had become hornless. Calves are now electrically dehorned at the bud stage and it is quite painless - they say! Occasionally tips of horns had to be sawn off, after fighting, or to prevent a twisted horn penetrating the animal's skull.

I never saw a Jay on our farm, probably because there was very little woodland cover for such a shy bird. A pair of Green Woodpeckers had their home in the ash tree on which the scarecrow was hung to scare the rooks; sometimes they could be seen from a bedroom window as they searched for grubs in the garden, and the echo heard of their short bursts of tapping as they looked for insects beneath dead bark. In the nearby ploughed field, known as The Mash, probably derived from marsh because it laid wet, I searched for the Peewits nest. The Peewit or Lapwing as it is called by some, is a lazy bird and makes no nest itself, but is satisfied to lay its eggs where a man's foot or horses had trodden. This bird puts on a great act of being wounded, flying up a few feet and falling down, trailing a broken wing to draw you away from the nest. One thing is certain; the nest will not be where the acrobatic act is being performed. The lapwing is a good friend of the farmer and feeds on grubs injurious to the growing corn. The eggs are camouflaged in darkest green with black blotches and easily missed. Nearby the lark will nest, taking advantage of the lapwings diversionary antics while it soars high into the heavens to sing yet again its song of happiness:-

Right happy bird so full of mirth
Mounting and mounting still more high
To meet morns sunshine in the sky
Ere yet it smiles on earth.
For who can cross green fields of corn
And see the skylark start to meet the day
And not feel more delighted on his way
Upon a summer morn.

John Clare.

The Yellow Hammer, known for it's song 'A little bit of bread and no cheese', nests in the wasteland bushes. On one occasion I wormed my hand and arm up through the prickly branches of a hawthorn bush, and as my fingers crept into the nest, a robber already there shot out down my arm and away. It was a weasel, the nest contained newly hatched young and he was having his evening meal.

The Yellow Hammer never makes a noise
but flies in silence from the noisy boys
The boys will come and take them every day
and still she lays as none were taken away.

John Clare

In an old hawthorn hedge bordering the Rector's field, known as Church Hole, there nested the one pair of magpies in the village. Their nest was made of prickly twigs, interwoven to a ball and covered so that only the bird knew where it's front and back doors were. I suppose, being such a thief itself, this bird trusts none other so besets itself around with thorn. Old Nati, on seeing a magpie fly by, would touch his forelock muttering low, so as not to be heard by the bird as it pass him by 'You old devil, you.!' I've always done likewise, just to be on the safe side.

I saw seven magpies in a tree
One for you and six for me
One for sorrow
Two for joy
Three for a girl
Four for a boy
Five for silver
Six for gold
Seven for a secret that's never been told
Eight is for heaven
Nine is for hell
And ten is for Satan his very self

(Folklore)

Towards the east end of the village where the brook joins the river there is a separately enclosed piece of land of some one and a half acres in extent known as the Swamp, for such it often was. This swamp was a paradise for small boys with it's fallen trees and jungle footpaths. It contained a boathouse and two rectangular fishponds. These were believed to have been there from Roman times and are similar to one at St. Ives which now, is simply shallow depression in a grass field. They would have been stocked with fish until required for the table, such 'keeps' were often situated near to monastic buildings in the early middle ages.

Willows having fallen and re-rooted hung their wispy branches over these ponds and it was there that the moorhen laid her clutch of eggs, pale ash colour spotted with lilac and chocolate markings. So temptingly just out of reach and causing many a wet foot in muddy boot. Only the brave removed boots and socks to wade knee deep for the prize, with rotting leaves and vegetation squelching up through toes. Here too, in an old pollarded willow some eight feet above the ground nested a wild duck. It was a regular nesting site year by year, and careful watch was kept to see when she started to lay, for her eggs provided many a clandestine meal in the Shepherd's hut.

The eggs lay hid in down and deeply prest
They counted more than thirty in the nest
They filled their hats with eggs and waded oe'r
And left the nest as quiet as before.

John Clare.

At home on this same old pollarded willow, and on the gnarled trunk of it's nearby ancient companion could be seen that shy and mouselike bird the Tree Creeper, making ever upward spirals round the trunk in it's search for grubs and insects, then down to the base and search again with his needle thin beak. Oh dear! Oh dear! Such a hungry family to feed, no time to stay and sing, just a quick chirp to mum then off again, a nestfull of babies, nine or even ten - and never still because he reckons to raise two families in the time that most birds take to raise one.

Beyond the swamp, between the flood dyke and the river lies a small meadow of about five acres in area. A man was once prevailed upon to mow the hay crop for twenty pence, whether by necessity or bravado is not known, but ever since that meadow has been known as 'Twenty-pence'.

Here in the reeds at the water's edge stands that one legged sentinel the Heron - lovely but lonely bird without his mate. Think not that he sleeps, as many an unsuspecting frog, or minnow, passing a 'stick' standing by the river bank has been so mislead. Before you could say 'Jack Robinson' the passer-by has been at the sharp end of stab and gulp with barely a neck feather ruffled, and waiting eye alert patient for the next innocent passer by. I've sat and watched him for an hour and seen him fly off into the setting sun, but never found his nesting site.

Neither did I ever see the nest of the Kingfisher, and rarely caught a glimpse of his swift blue arrow shape as he flashed and twisted along the brook into the reeds and gone.

What of the Jackdaw, no friend of my mother? Sooner or later one of the young family testing their flight feathers would return to the wrong chimney and fall into a room covering it with soot.

The Bullfinch, that dandy bird in his gay feathers, was no friend either, as he went from tree to tree in the orchard stealing the buds of this years crop of plums. Mother Partridge was a joy to watch on a summer evening cluck clucking softly as she kept in touch with he brood of fluff balls, hiding separate in the long grass, hidden from the piercing eye of predators of which there were many apart from the farmyard cat out looking for voles.

Much of the joy of nesting was not just the gaining of an egg to lay in the sawdust of an old cracker box, but sharing the secret of a bird's carefully chosen place in which to raise it's young, and to watch them as they grew until the day they left the nest. Even to share the sorrow as nest and young were destroyed by wind and flood, and by other creatures who were but fulfilling the role nature had intended them.

Enough, I think, of birds and nesting for there is much else to tell.

Lady-bird! Lady-bird! fly away home,
The field-mouse has gone to her nest,
The daisies have shut up their sleepy red eyes,
And the bees and the birds are at rest.

Lady-bird! Lady-bird! fly away now, -
to your house in the old willow tree,
Where your children, so dear, have invited the ant,
And a few cosy neighbours to tea.

Blackwoods, 1827

Chapter 21

Crows, Policemen and Harvest

"Thou hast provided for us a goodly earth:
Thou waterest her furrows,
Thou sendest rain into the little valleys thereof,
Thou makest it soft with the drops of rain,
and blessest the increase of it."

Psalm 65

Haymaking on Flaggholme, by Robert Winter (Sothebys)

My father never carried a gun. That is not to say we were denied the harvest rabbit, or a jugged hare in season; but to shoot birds out of the sky just for the fun of it was not part of his philosophy. He enjoyed the wild life on the farm. This attitude did not endear him to the so called gentry who were no longer allowed to walk the land, gun cocked and ready, as they had done under the previous owner. On a Sunday afternoon walk around the fields his most frequent comment would be 'look boy, look' - perhaps a covey of partridges put up with whirring wings to glide to safety in the distance, or, in the pasture field there would, to all appearances, be a mound of dried grasses to creep up on, then jumpback with surprise as at the last moment a hare sped out and away. These Sunday afternoon walks were rare and precious in hindsight; leaning on a field gate he once said 'A farmer's best work is done leaning on a gate' Wise words!

The Madingley crows were a mixed blessing, not being content with taking leather jacket and wireworm, they were also partial to both newly sown and later in season the ripened corn. There is an old country saying:-

Four seeds in a row.
One for the pigeon,
One for the crow,
One to rot and
One to grow.

They came in a flock with sunrise from Madingley Wood, a distance of five miles 'as the crow flies'. Between feeding they would rest in the branches of nearby ash trees, always facing the prevailing wind. To make life more difficult for them a scarecrow was made from old clothes stuffed with straw, and strung up among the dead branches of their favourite tree. Not many days had passed before Police Constable Creamer arrived on his bicycle to investigate a report received at St. Ives Police Station, from an agitated hiker, exhausted from running, that a man had hung himself in a tree at Holywell. The scarecrow had to come down!

At that time P.C. Creamer was our local Bobby, he came round the village on summer Sunday evenings on his bicycle. Stopping for a chat with residents, and sometimes bringing a swine movement order.

I had considerable respect for P.C. Creamer. I knew from the grapevine among boys, that he kept a glass alley up the fingers of his glove, and that it was unpleasant to get a whack round the ear for cheekiness or some minor misdemeanour. After all it was only a glove and complaint to a parent would receive but little sympathy and draw the comment 'serve you right'. Another member of the local force was P.C. Newby known as 'Mister' with affection, because that was the way he addressed everybody. Even to young lads it would be 'now off that crossbar Mister' or 'off the path Mister, I sha'nt tell you again', but of course he would when aggravated the next time.

The New Year was always a good time for rabbiting, often on a Sunday morning after milking the cows, feeding and watering the stock and horses the men from the farm cottages would set out with nets and ferrets to catch a few rabbits for the pot. All the well known bolt holes would be covered with a piece of netting before the ferret was put down the hole to flush out the rabbits - a quick dive when a net bulged, a sharp squeal followed by silence as rabbit number one was deftly gutted by razor sharp shut knife and laid out on the grass,

The last load — John Coulson pitching to Alf Leach,
'Bonny' between the shafts

to be sniffed at by the fox terrier, who before the morning was out would get his own chance to chase a rabbit escaping from an un-netted run. Sometimes the hungry ferret would corner a rabbit in a nesting burrow then he would kill and gorge himself; oft-times the line would catch in an old tree root beneath the hedgerow, then after considering how much line had been let out and the direction, digging would begin - which could mean an hour or more of hard work - but then, pleasure never is hard work! If all went well there would be an inquest on the morning's work over a pint in the pub, then home again for Sunday dinner, a quick nap and back to the farm-yard. One night a hungry fox ripped a hole in the wire netting of the run which held a flock of a dozen or so Rhode Island Red hens - the birds were precious to the chap who owned them. In the morning they were found beheaded and torn apart. In a joyous frenzy of blood and feathers the fox had whirled this way and that till all laid dead, then he picked up one and departed from the carnage to trot home to feed his family. Here lay his undoing, for tired from his efforts breath not yet regained, he needed to pause now and again to take fresh grip on his lifeless prey; leaving at each spot a feather or blood on the grass - a trail to his earthy home. Flushed out by the terrier and shot as he fled, I later saw him hanging by his brush on the chicken run gate as a warning to others should they think to do as he had done. Rabbits are the staple diet of foxes, but a hungry fox having a family to feed, may be forced to take risks, and pay the price if caught.

Harvest was the most exciting time for rabbits. As the reaping machine flailed its way around the corn field throwing out the sheaves, rabbits and hares are confined to an ever decreasing area of standing corn. First one would bolt then another, darting this way and that to avoid a body lunging with stick or stone. Often there was much shouting and laughter as men and boys chasing a different quarry collided in their eagerness. Sometimes the driver of the reaper with a 'Hold Ye' shout to the horses would jump from his seat and join the chase flinging his cap to confuse the quarry. If the area to be harvested for the day was not finished by dewfall all the game would have disappeared by morning. At this time of the year there would be fried rabbit for breakfast, with fried mushrooms if found along the headlands. Cold rabbit pies, pastry thick and crusty, covering joints of rabbit, chunks of fat port, all set in tasty jelly, to satisfy hungry harvest appetites.

As the corn ripened toward the time of harvest flocks of young sparrows would become a great nuisance, and could clear all the grain from the ears of corn to ten or fifteen feet from the hedgerow. Consequently, their nests were searched out beneath the eaves of farm buildings and destroyed. I doubt if it did any good because birds are most persistent in answering natures call to reproduce, and sparrows will have a nest rebuilt within a day or so of the old one being destroyed. We had a sparrow net; it spread out between two bamboo rods twelve feet in length. On a July or August evening my brother and I would set out for the cornfield as dusk approached. He being the stronger, had the net, we quietly approached a known roosting site along the hawthorn hedge. He on one side I on the other waiting for a softly whistled signal to thrash the hedge with a stick to flush out the birds; many of which would fly into the open net. Then 'wham' the rods brought together and the catch inspected in the half light. Sparrows met with summary execution, but other small birds such as linnets, finches, blackbirds and the occasional albino sparrow were set free. The same procedure would be followed further along the hedge, and sometimes in the stockyards where sparrows and starlings perched for the night on the hayracks above the mangers.

Chapter 22

The Shepherd's Hut Seal Money and Blackberry Pie

We had in the pasture a Shepherd's Hut. It had four cast iron wheels and could be horse drawn from one field to another. It contained all that a shepherd needed during lambing time, when he would need to be with his sheep for 24 hours of the day. It had a raised wooden bunk over a utensil cupboard, and above was a storage cupboard with sliding doors. There were windows, and a stable type door so that the top half could be opened independently of the lower half. Apart from it's practical use, it was a marvellous out of season place in which to play, and for my brother to skin his moles and conduct other post mortems. We had many a feast cooked on the small cast iron stove. Here I tested fried sparrow legs, wild duck and moorhen eggs, and various other delicacies according to season. Although never fully converted to these furtively held feasts I went along out of curiosity and brotherly love - sometimes stretched to the limit. Nearby was the orchard, containing apples, plums and pears of wonderful names and taste, to store secretly in the privacy of the hut's top cupboard. The apple Newton's Wonder keeps firm through to the following April - if allowed to do so. In years of plenty we would take a basket of these and poke them into the sides of haystacks to be retrieved as the need arose. Alas, like the squirrel we would forget the hiding place, or, most likely someone else would find them first. Corn in Egypt on a lucky day in mid winter!

The 2 horse power Massey-Harris hayloader at work.

Hay dealers were ever on the look-out for a good sweet scented hay, and none grew better than on the flower filled meadows of Holywell by the river Ouse. Mr. Hillyard was one such dealer - he bought hay for the Royal Mews and Police horses. With a hook ended iron rod he would probe to the centre of a haystack, twist and withdraw the rod with its wisp of hay caught up in the hook. This would be inspected, sniffed at to check for sweetness, or mould, making a further probe to settle any argument. A price would be agreed and a bargain struck. I liked to be around on such occasions. On a good day the clapping of the seller's hand against that of the buyer would be sealed by 'A florin for the boy'. On one such occasion the merits of a heifer had been long argued over and the sale was sealed by 'Half a sovereign to the boy then'. This seal money was afterwards divided between we three children. I learned that if a prospective buyer continued to find fault or 'crab' the article or beast for sale, you could be pretty certain he wanted it, and so hold out for a good price.

To return to apples: Beauty of Bath was the first dessert apple to ripen, ready to eat by late July. In August the ground beneath the trees would be deep in fallen fruit. Next would be the Somerset Quarendon, a smooth skinned flattish fruit deep red in colour and polished on jacket sleeve until it shone: Ready to be gathered and taken with other good things to be enjoyed on the river bank at St. Ives, between cheering home the rowing crews at the annual regatta. Then there was Blenheim Orange, raised at Woodstock in 1714 and beloved of my father not because it was Oxfordshire bred but because when blended with the wild blackberry it was best of all in a golden crusted pie - served with fresh dairy cream. 'No one makes a better pie than my girl' father would say, so we had plenty of them.

Annie Elizabeth, last of all the apples to be gathered, could be left on the tree until the first frost. Gathered quickly before the starlings found them, they would then be fit to eat until Codlins were ready in the following June.

There were others, ripening on gnarled old trees, names lost even then, but gathered in due season and laid out on straw in the apple loft - to tease your taste buds as they laid in rows in the scented darkness. and accessible only by ladder through a trap door.

I will mention just one plum for its beautiful name; 'Belle de Louvain', as round as a golf ball, with a bloom that would take ones finger print, and unbeatable when fully ripe and encased in a suet crusted pudding. It was at Louvain that Dick Reynolds was to lay down his life for his country.

These were busy days in the farmhouse kitchen. Jam and Jelly making: Preserving fruit in jars; chutneys, and onions to pickle while wiping streaming eyes.

It was harvest, and autumn, and preparation for the hard days of winter to come.

Chapter 23

Song Birds for London

Time was when I was free as air,
The thistle downy feed my fare,
My drink the morning dew;
I perched at will on ev'ry spray,
My form genteel, my plumage gay,
My strain for ever new.

But gaudy plumage, sprightly strain,
And form genteel were all in vain,
And of a transient date;
For, caught and caged, and starved to death,
In dying sighs my little breath,
soon passed the wiry grate.

Thanks, gentle swain, for all my woes,
And thanks for this effectual close,
And cure of ev'ry ill!
More cruelty could none express;
And I, if you had shewn me less,
Had been your pris'ner still.

William Cowper (1733-1800)

William Cowper lived for part of his life at Huntingdon before moving to Olney where he lived close to his friend John Newton, and let hares run free in his house and large garden. It is clear from this poignant poem that the capture of wild birds and the caging of them is by no means new and it continues to this day.

In late summer an old bird trapper would arrive in the village and set up his nets and traps in Coldham's field, just as the thistles which grew there in great patches were ripening and the seed ready to break. These thistles were a great attraction to the flocks of young Goldfinch, and other seed eating birds. In among the nets would be one or two decoy birds, well supplied with seed and water in airy wicker cages. The hapless captives would unwittingly sing their siren songs, to fool their fellow creatures into a false sense of security and inevitable capture.

The old trapper was out to catch the Goldfinch for its song and its colour, but was not averse to taking Linnets as well.

After a morning's work the captured birds would be sent on the afternoon 'milk train' from St. Ives railway station bound for the London market, to be sold as singing birds. I wonder how brief their song, and their lives, in those little cages after the freedom of the skies at Holywell.

I recall an occasion when this old man set his traps in the Vineyard, our field next to Coldham's, and was turned out by my furious father. Even so he would sneak in a net and sometimes get away with it. This was the only field on the farm in which the creeping thistle was allowed to flourish unhindered, and I like to think that it was left to go wild and draw the birds away from the danger next door.

I heartily disliked anything to do with London. On going with my mother to visit an ancient great aunt, I had once seen dray horses stabled beneath the arches close by Kings Cross station with barely room to lift their heads, and compared them to our horses able to roll in the grass and kick their legs up in the air after a days work, whinnying and snorting with joy. I could not see much joy beneath the arches after a hard day's work on the London street.

Hanging by their necks in rows outside a poulterer's shop I had seen starlings, peewits, blackbirds and rooks along with game birds. I could hardly believe that these were for people to eat, but then I had seen a boy of my own age with neither shoes or socks, begging a halfpenny for opening the door of a Lyons Teashop.

I suppose on getting home I kept on about the unusual sights until in desperation, my mother said 'I can't tell you why, one day you will understand'. That usually brought the conversation to an end, but on this occasion, which made it memorable, my father said 'If they keep digging those tunnels under London, one day, the whole lot will collapse'.

That was in 1929. On that occasion I believe his judgement was not sound and I suggest the danger has passed!!

Chapter 24

The Brook

Rise up my love, my fair one, and come away,
For lo, the Winter is past, the rain is over and gone;
the flowers appear on the earth!
the time of the singing bird is come.

Song of Solomon 2 v 12

The brook which ran through our fields held a fascination for me and I could often be found on its banks. First a walk down Conger Lane between the hedgerows where white and purple violets grow, and Lords and Ladies sheltering beneath the hawthorn hide their berries which in autumn would turn bright red, in danger sign of their deadly poison. The lane ended at the foot-bridge leading to Parsons Drove. On the handrails local lads idly carved their initials - the more daring carved hearts pierced with an arrow, and dared the thrill of carving the initials of a loved one for all to see. One evening I was idly leaning on the rail watching a water rat busy about his homemaking in the bank just above water level when with scarce a movement, other than an arrow headed ripple of the water, there passed beneath me and under the bridge an otter. I hurried home to tell. Of course, no-one believed me, but it was true just the same. Within a few years the brook was to become polluted by industrial sewage from St. Ives, but it was then clear water. Sometimes in full flood, sometimes little more than a trickle. In a few places the brook had a gravelley bottom and watercress could be picked and taken to the greengrocer on the way to school. In a low lying area loved by the pigs there grew Teasel with prickly stem and heads banded in little pink flowers. The meadow beyond the brook was carpeted with cowslips in the spring. The name cowslip is derived fromthe Old English word cuslyppe or cuslop, meaning cowdung or cowpat, later to become with some delicacy, cowslip. The Primula Veris found that an old cowpat was the ideal medium for it's tiny seeds to germinate and flourish. On a sunny afternoon we would all go to the meadow taking sandwiches, cake and lemonade, to fill baskets with the delicately perfumed flower heads for our mother to turn into wine. This and the parsnip were the most prized of the home made wine; one delicate the other potent. A lady in the village would give us sixpence for a pint pot filled with just the yellow flowers, to make an infusion of delicately flavoured cowslip tea.

It takes a very, very, long time to fill a pint pot with cowslip flowers and if not delivered immediately they would shrink as you watched them, and with them the sixpence. In the late summer the brook would be bounded in a Chelsea like blaze of red hot poker, properly named Purple Loose-strife, and here too grew Meadowsweet in profusion. Best of all, and surely well up in the top ten of Holywell wild flowers with its pale blue and yellow eyed dainty flowers is the Water Forget-me-Not. They flourished along the banks of the brook, reflecting in the water as they swayed in the breeze. I wonder did the lover fall in and drown, as he offered the pretty flowers to his lady or was he pushed! The scene is set for the outstretched hand to offer the sweet bouquet to his love with those immortal words 'forget-me-not' as he vanished beneath the silent water. Here too Narcissus might have fallen in love with his reflection in the clear water.

In between the beds of Forget-me-Not grew the fragrant lilac-coloured Wild Mint, and along this stretch of water by the field known as Water Gate, flew the Dragon-Fly, and the Swallow in weaving flight to catch an evening meal of insects. Here too, the Common Blue, and the Little Orange Tipped butterflies were a common sight in spring.

The ground begins to rise to the farmstead and the village, 22ft above sea level at its highest point. Below the farmyard buildings is an ancient rabbit warren and a badger set. In the scratched-out gravel I found a shard of pottery, identified as Roman. The ever flowing water from the Holy Well by the Church, trickles down a mini stream to join the brook in Church Hole, beneath a foot-bridge. The brook flows on beside Flaggholme to join the river. Here, between the brook and river grows a line of willows, pollarded year by year for fencing rails and posties (the plural for post in local dialect). Bill Leach could split a willow pole dead centre from end to end, using pressure on the billhook this way and that to prevent the crack running out.

In this swampy ground grew masses of Golden Kingcups, to be joined by acres of Lady's Smock, with many headed flowers of lilac and white. Some call this lovely flower Cuckoo Flower because it blooms for the most part in April and May when the Cuckoo sings without stammering, but I prefer the simple name of Milkmaid, in memory of my Grandmother. In the drier parts of the big meadow the common Buttercup grew. Is there any child who has not waited with upturned chin to know if the bright yellow flower reflects the love of butter - and is there one that has been disappointed as the yellow pollen, in proof, is wiped off by tiny fingers?

There were fish in the brook and eels too, but the fish I knew came in boxes by post from Yarmouth, or rush baskets from Grimsby. Fishing played no significant part in my childhood. The river bank was my boundary, but sometimes walking by the brook to school I would look under the arched bridge leading to Flaggholme for a sight of the old Pike who frequently lay there in the cool of a summer's day. Many times from the bridge I have seen the green and black ringed Grass Snake, making his way upstream just beneath the surface of the water, with sinuous rhythmic movement of his four-foot length.

The snakes laid their rubbery white eggs, glued together in clusters of 20 or more a few inches down in the self-generating heat of the farmyard manure heap. On a sunny day in high summer they could be seen hatching out, some could be assisted as they poked their little heads out of the tough membrane of the egg; Little six inch miniatures of their parents, wriggling away to find safety in the grass which grew green and rank around the oozing sides of the heap. The carrion crow and the magpie were the give-away sign of hatching. Destined to crawl on their bellies all their life these little snakes had but small chance of reaching adulthood and enjoying a swim in the brook for they had many predators to hide from. Farm boys know early in life about the birds and the bees, not furtively, but as a natural event of every day life, even so, it was and is to me a mystery how the eggs become fertilised and laid. When blackberrying quietly on the sunny side of a hedge early on a September morning these quite harmless snakes could frequently be seen sunning themselves on the short grass by the hedgerow, and occasionally shedding their skin.

To return to the brook; mention must be made of the elegant yellow Flag Iris. There is no finer picture than a dragon fly resting or drying his wings on the flower of the Iris. If the Forget-me-Not is the prettiest of the brook flowers, then the Iris must be the most regal. The Reed-Mace Bulrush seemed to grow most where the brook widened in its course to swirl round a Willow tree encroaching from the bank as it put on years, and everywhere the dock would grow, adding to the glow of autumn colour.

The bane of my father's life was the Creeping Thistle, which revelled in the soft damp soil by the brook, closely followed in dislike was the Stinging-nettle. Both were loved by the butterflies but, on the whole, were the most disagreeable of the plants along the brook.

In the still water between the mouth of the brook and the main stream of the river there grew a profusion of the little yellow Water Lily, sometimes called 'brandy bottle' because the seed pods are shaped like a flask, their leaves so dense upon the water that a Moorhen and her chicks could scurry home to reed-bed safety without once needing to take to water.

Forget Me Not

Thy name is Love's own poetry,
Heart-born, and of the eye begot,
Pleading for aye, 'Remember me;'
Replying, 'I'll Forget thee not.'

Thy blue dost emblem Constancy,
Love never more to be forgot,
And By the streams grows everywhere,
Unchanged through every changing year.

Here in sunshine, there in shade,
Where embower'd streamlets brawl,
It ever stands, and seems afraid
When the shadows on it fall;

But in warm sunshine when array'd,
It never knoweth fear at all.
So Love, when there is none to cherish,
Neglected stands, and soon will perish.

So when the sun's hid from the flower,
And warm golden beams forsake it,
It bows its head, and from that hour
Prays only unto Death to take it.

Anon.

David Tabbitt's house, 'Oak Cottage' with cows grazing the roadside verges

Chapter 25

"Beauty," a Shire Horse

When my harness was taken off, I did not know what I should do...
first - whether to eat the grass, or roll over on my back, or have a gallop across the meadow out of sheer spirits at being free...
Anna Sewell, 'Black Beauty'

By the eleventh summer of my life I believe I knew every nook and cranny on the farm, many of which hold special memories that are with me to this day, and several involve my good friend Beauty, the Shire Horse. She knew all my childhood secrets, passing sorrows and ambitions, was a good listener, and showed interest by cocking her ear. In my early years I was certain she could speak if only she would make the effort. As I grew in age so I grew in strength, and was able in a small way to play my part and contribute to the work on the farm. The *Punch* characterisation of the farm worker as a country yokel, sucking a straw, may make a good cartoon, but is nothing less than a travesty of the truth: (e.g. Angry car driver, whose vehicle had become submerged in the waters of a ford crossing, "You said the water in this ford was not very deep". Country yokel "Ah! well, you see that only come half way up my 'ole ducks").

The fact is, there are so many facets to life on a mixed dairy farm that one is never finished learning, and most of the knowledge which is essential in the care of animals and to their well-being, is absorbed by working alongside others from birth and following their example. In this way knowledge has been handed down through the generations and is, as they say, in the blood. I cannot recall being taught many of the small tasks I performed. How to harness Beauty or how to attach her to the cart or other implement; how to arrange sheaves so they would not slip and fall when jolting on the way to the stackyard. But these and many other tricks of the trade came with daily use.

Beauty was the only horse I was allowed to work alone with. She was without doubt the first love of my life, always willing, intelligent, and gentle. No head flinging, storming off tantrums with her, or refusing to back between the shafts of the cart for another day's work as some of her stable companions were liable to do. Having been to a circus, I recall lying on the ground in front of her feet, and trying to get her to step over me as I had seen performed in the circus act, but she would have none of it, hard though I tugged on the halter.

One of my earliest boyhood jobs in the harvest field was to be 'soldier boy', a derivation from 'hold-ye' boy. With a click of the tongue, hand on the bridle, one shouted 'hold-ye' to warn the man arranging the sheaves on the cart to hold tight, and not be thrown as the cart jolted forward over the rough ground to the next stook in readiness for it to be pitched up, and so build up the load. Sometimes there would be a stook on either side of the cart, depending on the bounty of the harvest. Some horses are difficult, and a carthorse's hoof brought down sharply on a boy's foot can be painful - very painful! Beauty could judge when the cart she was pulling was opposite the next stook to be loaded and at the sound of 'hold-ye,' would move forward without need for hand to bridle, leaving the hold-ye boy free to give a hand with loading the sheaves.

The Muck-Cart, by Joe Godderidge

Once with Boxer I lost a load of hay because he would not keep to the centre of the lane, and had to endure chaffing from the men because of it. I never lost a load with Beauty, although once a load was too wide for the field gateway and we got stuck much to everyone's amusement, but she could hardly be blamed for that.

Beauty loved a piece of fruit cake, smuggled from the tin in the pantry, not always easy, but it was years before mother found out, and then to my delight she would often say 'I've packed a bit of cake for Beauty as well'. On a Saturday morning in winter I would load up a cart with manure from the stock-yard and take it to the farm 'muck-heap' in the vineyard, then load up with mangolds from the arable field and bring them back to go through the root cutter, ready to be mixed with chaff and meal, or linseed cake for the afternoon feeding of the dairy Shorthorn cows and the horses.

On a Saturday morning in June 1934 Beauty and I were sent to carry out a final raking of Noble's field by the river where the hay crop had been carted during the week. The hay-rake had a ten foot sweep of pointed semi-circular arms close together to gather up the hay and hold it until released in windrows by the operator. To achieve this the operator, who sat on a shaped metal seat behind the horse whom he controlled by reins, pressed down hard with his right foot on a cantilevered arm which then raised the whole sweep of the rake and released its load of hay. It was a matter of pride to keep the windrows straight (or of ridicule, if this was not achieved; 'Ah boy, you could catch a rabbit there alright he would get that dizzy'). Then with a clang the rake dropped back without pause in the progress across the field. This particular field was subject to minor whirlwinds which sucked the hay up ten or fifteen feet into the air before collapsing. Consequently, there was more hay than usual for the final raking. The upshot was that I spaced the rows too far apart, and to give the rake sufficient height in releasing it's load, the mechanism had to be pressed downwards to its maximum depth. This I could achieve only by rising from the seat, standing up with my right foot on the pad and pressing down with the full weight of my body, then dropping back on the seat. I achieved this manoeuvre several times before carelessness and disaster struck - my foot slipped off the pad I missed the seat and tumbled down between the rake and Beauty's hind legs. She should have bolted. Most horses would have been 'off' in fright, and I caught between flying hooves, iron wheels, and hay rake teeth! But she stood right there, until I extricated myself and went to her head and embraced her. Why did she stand still? How did she know? All I know is that I could have been badly injured, but I lived and learned the lesson that pride in one's work is one thing, but foolishness is something different.

There are other less dramatic tales of Beauty, like the day she tipped me in the pond. I was riding her bare-back from the stable, where she had eaten, across to the pasture, when she stopped by the pond for a drink. Perhaps she objected to getting her feet wet, because suddenly I was awakened from my day-dream and sliding down her neck, and over her head for a ducking. I like to think it was an accident of gravity, and not one of equine wickedness.

When Beauty lost a shoe or they became worn, I was allowed to take her to the farrier in Standen's Yard in East Street, St. Ives. While she was being shod I would follow mother's instruction and go to Mr. Wright's Barber Shop nearby for a fourpenny haircut. There was usually a queue both for the blacksmith's work and at the barber's. This gave me opportunity to catch up on the comics of which Mr. Wright always had a good supply, so a shop full of customers was a welcome sight. I never liked to see the sizzling hot shoe nailed on the Beauty's hoof, although to her it was quite painless as it gave off a cloud of acrid smelling smoke. She was no thoroughbred racehorse, but that did not diminish the pride I felt in riding her through the town as we journied to and from the farriers. Before leaving home she had been subjected to a good currycombing and brushdown. Her black mane and long tail hair always looked well and shone on these occasions.

One of my favourite stories, over which I shed a good many tears was Anna Sewell's 'Black Beauty'. My Beauty had a white star on her forehead, and a few grey hairs among the black of her main. She may only have been a carthorse, but she had an eventful life. The broad arrow branded with searing hot iron on her buttocks showed that she had been conscripted into the army, as had many thousands of horses during the great War of 1914 - 1918. Army Veterinary Agents toured the farms of East Anglia and selected the strong young horses needed to help in the fight against the Hun. There is no telling where she had been or what sights she had seen in service for her country. My father bought her at the Banbury Horse Fair in 1920, the dealer said 'she's a beauty', and that is how she came to be named.

The last I saw of Beauty was her being led away from the farm by her purchaser at the farm sale. The Auctioneer did not dwell, and the hammer fell like doom to the highest bidder at £5 (it is not a misprint). I felt a Judas, and ashamed that her trust and loyalty had been so betrayed. Even now it is difficult to describe my feelings on that day except, perhaps, to say that when my father died I wanted to give way to tears and could not. When I watched Beauty being led away I wanted to stay dry eyed but went to her stall in the stable, where her scent remained, and wept.

I am bound to question 'Of all the dumb creatures of this world, which is man's best friend? Is it the dog, or the horse?' Today, I must surely be on the side of the horse.

Joe Godderidge, the Norfolk artist, works with heavy horses on his twenty acre dairy farm, and with the day's work behind him turns to the easel and captures their movements on canvas. 'I have worked with heavy horses most of my life' he says 'and most people develop a great respect, if not a downright love for them, you could not want to work with anyone better.' His team of Shires, Blossom, Anna, and Buster provide the horse-power for ploughing, harrowing, hayraking, and carting on the farm, and it is those every-day scenes that he strives to capture on canvas — mud and all!

Start of the Day, by Joe Godderidge

I have no picture of Beauty to display, but thanks to Joe and his passion for these gentle giants I can still give them tribute in these pages.

Chapter 26

Beagling

There is a kind of dog of mighty fame
For hunting, worthier of a fairer fame
By painted Britons brave in war they're bred,
Are Beagles called, and to the chase are led
Their bodies small

(The Greek writer, Oppian, 100 A.D.)

My father would not allow shooting parties on his land, which led him into some unpopularity with the local gentry. Colonel Ramsbotham, on behalf of the shooting fraternity, remonstrated with him, to no avail, and said 'It was jolly unsporting to deny them walking the manor lands as they had done while Mr. Churton was the landowner'. The colonel lived at 'The Anchor', previously a public house, and we often met as I made my way to school. I was impressed by his regular 'Hello young fella' followed by a grumbling 'hard man your father' or some similar remark.

The Trinity Foot Beagle Pack, photographed by Alan Neale

However, my father did allow the winter time visits by the Trinity Foot Beagles to continue. I think he had a soft spot for these brave little dogs. The Beagle is probably one of the oldest hounds of the chase, being so small that they hunt by scent rather than by sight. The quarry is usually the common brown hare, and a wily creature 'she' is, (The hare is generally referred to by country folk as 'she' for some obscure reason). The hare usually tends to work round in circles, doubles back or springs to one side and lies low. She will lie in among sugar beet or swedes until the last seconds of approaching danger, then up and away, to the heightened, joyous and melodious cry of these jolly carefree dogs. Old Nati was said to be able to creep up on a hare lying in its form of long grasses and break its back with one swipe of his stick - I wonder how many empty 'forms' he swiped!

The hare, being on her own ground, takes every advantage of this knowledge to dart through a gap in the hedge, too low for the hounds to follow and run along a road, or along a watery ditch where the scent does not hold. As often as not she wins the day by these clever manoeuvres.

After three or four hours, huntsmen, dogs and followers will have had enough exercise and excitement, and make a tired way home. A few hours on a February day tramping the heavy clay of an arable field calls upon muscles of which one is otherwise unaware.

The Beagle deserves this special spot in a history of Holywell. It is a reminder of those distant days when the heath and woodland of the parish resounded to the Huntsman's horn and the cry of hounds in the chase. The saddest thing of all is to see these great little dogs, which by definition are pack animals, treated as pets, straining at the end of a lead, when they want nothing more than to be nose down, tail erect and away after some nose twitching scent.

'To plain with well-bred Beagles we repair,
and trace the mazes of the circling hare.'

Pope, 1688

Chapter 27

Pocket Money

We were not given regular weekly pocket money. There was very little at Holywell for a child to spend money on. There were no shops. Beatty Carter at the White Horse sold marshmallows which were quite delectable but only an occasional treat. The village shop at Needingworth, next to the old Ducks Nest pub, was a wonderland.

One year a fruit set, of a bowl and six dishes decorated with a crinolined lady in a garden scene, was displayed for sale in the window. This seemed ideal for our mother's birthday on 26th September. My sister and I walked to Needingworth several times to make sure it was still there. The difficulty was the price of 7/6d (37½ pence) - a lot of money at that time. Blackberries begin to ripen in September and this source of income was to be our means of raising such a large sum. At the beginning of the season blackberries could be sold to the shops, or to Toby Course in North Road, St. Ives at fourpence a pound, but as they became more plentiful the price dropped to two pence. The best went to Chivers at Histon for jam or jelly making, and later in the season they were tipped in to tubs and went to make dye. Mrs. Course was very fair and if the berries were carefully picked, without stalks, or leaves, or unripe fruit, we would get top price. We would often be out by 7 a.m., but even then Belinda Smith would sometimes have beaten us to a well-liked hedge-row. Being quite a tall boy, I could reach berries that were beyond Belinda's grasp and like us she would pick to come again. Sometimes a good spot would be ruined for the season by townees breaking the branches to reach the fruit, and smashing at the hedge with sticks. We bought the fruit set that year. Mother was delighted, and I thought it was marvellous that such a thing could be obtained simply by picking wild fruits that were there for anyone to gather.

Once I was peppered with spent lead shot; A Mr Vawser had fired his 12 bore at a rabbit which I had unknowingly flushed out to the opposite side of the hedge on which I was gathering blackberries. The pellets stung but no harm was done either to me or the rabbit.

A year or so later whilst quietly blackberrying in Benjamins, the orchid field, now unfortunately vandalised for gravel, I heard what I thought was a child whimpering then it developed to a squeal of real terror. I moved a few paces and witnessed a small drama through a gap in the hedge. Facing me was a rabbit hunched and petrified in

fear; facing it and back to me was a stoat (or maybe a weasel), head alert and perfectly poised. As I watched the stoat struck and had the rabbit by the throat tumbling over and over into a bed of nettles.
I guess that is not the pretty side of nature!

The road leading from Needingworth to Holywell in the 1920's was little more than a single cart track, and beside it a footpath. Both were maintained by David Coulson the parish roadman. At intervals along the grass verge were heaps of stones and gravel which, as wear took place, were rammed into ruts and holes caused by the passage of cart and waggon wheels. Along the centre of the road it was not unusual to see grass growing. However, by the 1930's the road surface was much improved. Hot tar spread by large cans was poured on to the road surface, covered by shovel with gravel, and made firm by the steam driven roller.

The age of the motor car was coming to Holywell and there were three in the village. The Rector had a Renault, Jimmy Hodkinson the poultry farmer had a vehicle known as the Bean, and my father had a Rover with which I became the more familiar. It had a canvas roof, celluloid windows apart from the glass windshield; a running board on either side, wooden wheels and beaded edged tyres; It had gaited gears and was swing-started by a handle beneath the radiator.

The car held an almost unlimited number of passengers, quite often five children and four adults. Petrol was delivered weekly by Pratts in 2 gallon cans - it was quite straightforward; a dozen or so cans were stacked by the wall in the garage and the delivery man simply replaced the empty cans by full ones.

My father usually drove the car. The normal method of learning was to 'have a go'; my mother did quite well at her first attempt, but on the second and being somewhat confused by the gears momentarily forgot how to stop the vehicle. She did so by running the car on to one of David Coulson's stone heaps. The ever faithful carthorse Beauty was brought to the rescue and towed the car off the heap, a circumstance mother was never allowed to forget when passing that particular stone heap.

George Reynolds usually got the car ready for use and mended the punctures etc. (no easy task with beaded tyres). One day, instead of simply being reversed out of the garage, it was facing the right direction. 'Who turned the car round' asked mother, 'I did' said George, 'Well, if you can do that we had better get you a licence' she said. So off they went to Huntingdon and got George his licence to drive. On leaving the town mother said 'now you can drive home' which he did, wondering as they drove along if he would be able to steer the car safely through the gates leading in to the drive at Holywell. All went well, and from then on George had the added duty of Chauffeur and drove the car as often as was needed.

The grass verges of the highway and the expanse of grass along the front of the village were grazed by Bill Prior's herd of dairy cows. Dorothy Ibbott of Holywell was a cow minder and it was her job to see that the cattle kept to the verges and were returned for afternoon milking to the farmstead known as The Huts at the top of Pound Hill, Needingworth. Sometimes a cowgirl would look after animals belonging to more than one owner. Dorothy died quite young from pneumonia, quite probably caused by getting cold and wet in day long inclement weather while minding the cattle.

Dorothy was carried to her last resting place in Holywell churchyard by her cousins the boys of Tabbitt. She lies alongside her sister Betty. Betty who had been so full of life; I recall seeing her on a summer afternoon shortly before her death, lying in a bedlike conveyance and being slowly wheeled round the village, perhaps the last lingering look at the scenes so familiar during her short life.

On Saturdays I had a flower round in St. Ives, and my brother had a vegetable round. He had worked his round up so that he needed the pony and cart. The proceeds from these ventures went to the farm, but anything grown on our own garden plot we could keep. I did very well with bunched radishes. One had to be up early in the morning to cut and bunch the flowers, and gather any fruit and vegetables which were available for sale according to the time of year. There were always a few swedes growing among the mangolds for cattle consumption, and a few of these, although heavy to carry on the bicycle, always sold well.

This was hungry work, and one pennyworth of stale cakes from Stiles Fountain Cafe, or of left over Friday night chips from Fred Lowery's Fish and Chip Shop, in the Broadway, were both good gap fillers. An alternative on a good day, was a fourpenny pork pie from the Co-op this was considered a better buy than the sixpenny jelly filled pie from Stiles'.

At Mrs Simpson's sweet shop along the Waits, one anxiously watched the scales as a pennyworth of Sharp's toffees were weighed out, usually six toffees but seven if you were in luck. As I usually had a pocketful of apples I was not often tempted to sweets.

Books were a different matter - in school holidays I would cycle to Cambridge and go round the second-hand bookstalls. My favourite stall was at Heffer's in Petty Cury, where hundreds of books were in racks under an archway and one could spend hours there without being asked to buy. It was always a thrill to find and open the cover of an Everyman Library series book and read the words 'Everyman, I will go with thee, and be thy guide in thy most need to go by thy side', and then, 'A tale which holdeth children from play and old men from the chimney corner'

For a few pence I could pick up hours of adventure to take home with me. 'Lorna Doone' kept me awake for many nights with a torch beneath the sheets. 'Ben Hur', 'The Mill on the Floss' and many more wonderful tales thrilled me, too.

Miss Edith Mary Deane retired from business in London to enjoy an idyllic life in the country. She bought a horse and wellington boots and Berry House at Holywell. She had a weakness for auction sale bargains and filled her barns with them, to the great happiness of the mouse population. Unfortunately, magic though Holywell was, the reality did not quite fit the dream, and the horse had to go. Nevertheless she enjoyed her retirement; she became a well loved eccentric as she walked the lanes in her wellington boots until called to higher service. For several years I was her garden boy and mouse catcher at four pence an hour, later increased to sixpence. I was also garden boy for Mrs. 'Bobby' Fraser at the same rate, but due to a peculiar irregularity of the Fraser clock the average rate worked out at about two pence. Gardening is rather like painting the Forth Bridge it is never finished, so for the country boy it provided a regular source of income.

Added to gardening was the income from rabbit skins, mushrooms, crab apples, watercress, fallen apples, fairings etc. so we managed quite well, and in one year I saved up sufficient to pay five pounds for a new Raleigh Roadster bicycle. I was very proud of this bicycle and as I grew older cycled to Hunstanton several times for a dip in the sea, tea on the beach then home again.

My mother and sister would have taken the afternoon rail excursion which left St. Ives at 2 p.m. and returned from Hunstanton at 8 p.m. The train was always crowded, having picked up passengers at all the fen villages en route. It was like 'rush hour' on arrival at Hunstanton, with a happy throng of buxom fen mothers, and with hundreds of excited children waving buckets and spades, and making a dash for the sands to build sand castles paddle in the sea and ride the donkeys.

Chapter 28

Sunday

Tis sweet to hear a brook,
Tis Sweet to hear the Sabbath Bell;
Tis sweet to hear them both at once,
Deep in the woody dell.

Coleridge

Sunday always started well at the Manor, with the sight and sound of sausages sizzling on the kitchen range. It was the one day of the week when all the family could gather round the kitchen table and take breakfast together — an hour later than usual so that father could be in from his early morning round of the farm. We offered a simple Grace, with some argument as to whose turn it was to say the words:-

Thank you for the world so sweet,
Thank you for the food we eat,
Thank you for the birds that sing,
Thank you God for everything.

The Tranquil Ouse, by Robert Winter

We could then tuck in to the sausages and crisply fried bubble and squeak. In winter there would be steaming creamy porridge, with brown sugar and golden syrup. Then, 'Thank God for my breakfast, and please may I get down?'

Most of the essential work with the livestock, milking and feeding of the animals would have been completed by breakfast time, but always the unexpected was happening. A cow having a difficult calving, a broken fence and animals straying, piglets loose, someone bringing a sow to visit the boar, chickens hatching, Always something!

So far as we children were concerned it would soon be time for a good scrub up and to don our Sunday best to the sound of Church bells. God's acre was just the other side of the stackyard wall, so in a manner of speaking, God was our neighbour!

It was considered very bad manners to be late for Church, and equally bad to be seen running on Sunday, so careful timing was called for. I regret to say that I understood very little of the service at that time, but I loved the rich tones of the organ, the singing, and above all the stained glass window. At the close of service the Rector took us children across to the Rectory for 'a talk' and it was here that I first became acquainted with my Guardian Angel - to whom honour. Then it was a quick dash for home, (forgetting the 'no running' rule), yorkshire pudding and roast beef, the yorkshire always cooked under the meat and eaten first with plenty of thick hot onion gravy. There was a golden crusted pie and custard for dessert. Those were the days!

At one time my brother Henry had a pet Harvest Mouse which by constant handling became quite tame, and lived in a converted wooden box with the words Reckitts and Coleman Starch printed on the side. Consequently the mouse became known as Reckitts. Apart from wash-day the hutch, which contained all that a harvest mouse could possibly need, was safely hidden in a corner of the wash-house. Amongst other bits and pieces considered useful to a harvest mouse, it had a miniature corn stook similar to those in top field from which it was a refugee, and appeared to be quite at home in these surroundings.

One Sunday Henry, for reasons best known to himself, decided to take Reckitts to church. The mouse was not discovered at our pre-church inspection by mother and we set off with Reckitts safely settled in my brother's jacket pocket - where he spent a good deal of his time when not in his wash-house home. All went well until, during the sermon, Henry decided to take the mouse out of his pocket for a game of passing from one hand to the other, which normally Reckitts enjoyed. But then, uncharacteristically, Reckitts lost his footing and fell to the floor, lost his bearings, and pranced about in the aisle. It was not long before ladies whispering 'a mouse', 'there's a mouse' became audible above the Rector's drone. Henry became agitated, and fearing for Reckitts' life, got up from his seat and after a few abortive attempts scooped the mouse up and made for the church door. There, with great presence of mind, he popped Reckitts in his pocket while pretending to throw him outside, and returned to his pew. At the close of service he became something of a hero for his 'bravery'.

It was inevitable that after a few days news of the exploit reached mother's ears. Henry was called 'over the coals', and Reckitts life of luxury came to an end. He was returned to the wild, where for all I know he happily lived out the remainder of his life.

No ball games were played on Sunday. As reading was my favourite past-time - often leading me into trouble - this was no hardship, and I could get my head into a book without being remonstrated for neglecting some duty or other. Once I was severely scolded for picking blackberries on the way home from church and my mother refused to accept them into the house, the fact that someone else might have picked them before Monday did not carry any weight. One of my daily duties was to collect up the eggs, including those laid astray beneath the hedgerow and, I recall, my thinking got quite confused over the right and wrong of blackberrying and that of collecting up the eggs on the 'day of rest'.

It was a special treat if I was asked by my father to accompany him on a walk, or a visit to a neighbouring farmer - it was usually my brother's privilege, he being that much older and expected to follow in father's footsteps. We often had friends to tea on a Sunday. The news that so-and-so would be coming to tea would be greeted with groans, or expressions of joy, according to the level of behaviour expected of us. One dear lady whose visits were enjoyed, on being pressed to have a little more of some tea-time delicacy would eventually come to the point of saying 'I've had an ample sufficiency, thank-you', much to our delight.

My father and Mr. Jack Barter were good friends during the time that our two families lived in close proximity at St. Ives, and this friendship continued after our move to Holywell. Mr. Barter budded several varieties of rose on to hedgerow briars planted in the garden at the Manor, and these together with Primula Auricula which he also cultivated, provided many a button hole which my father displayed on his jacket, rarely going to market without a flower of some kind. Jack kept a cow, some pigs, and poultry in the orchard at Rheola so there was much to discuss when he came over to Holywell on a Sunday morning with his airedale dog Bess running alongside. Bess was trained to stay by his cycle as it stood in the drive. Mr & Mrs Barter had twin daughters, Faith, and Olive who were the same age as myself, and later young Jack arrived. It was a special treat for the girls and for my sister and myself, for we rarely had visitors of our own age, when they came over from St. Ives for the day. George would bring them in the milk float when returning from the morning milk round. We had great times playing croquet, to our own rules, on the lawn, and other games in the house or on the farm according to the weather.

Sometimes we would all pile aboard the Rover car and go off to the seaside at Hunstanton, stopping for a picnic beneath the pine trees at

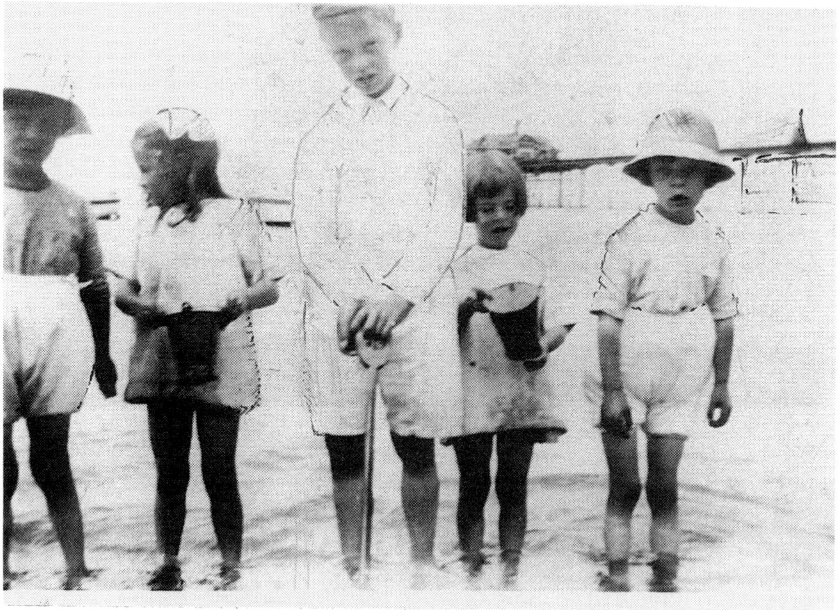

Olive and Faith Barter, with we three at Hunstanton

Sandringham. The journey seemed to take several hours and there was always competition, miles before Hunstanton, jumping up and down to be first in spying the sea,and with many false alarms. These were jolly occasions only brought to an end when my father died, and Mrs Barter also died quite young.

There is no better place on a Sunday than within the sound of church bells as they ring out their message across the meadows and centuries. If you look for the heart of England, you need to look no further than a spring or summer day by the church at Holywell. Yet there is more to the peaceful scene than the enjoyment of hearing the bells as they ring, and it must surely be to heed their calling, join the countless throng of boys and girls, men and women, who for a thousand years and more have passed this way to enter the house of God and there to bring their hopes and fears, their joys and sorrows. To kneel, where T.S. Elliot speaking of Little Gidding, says 'prayer is valid'.

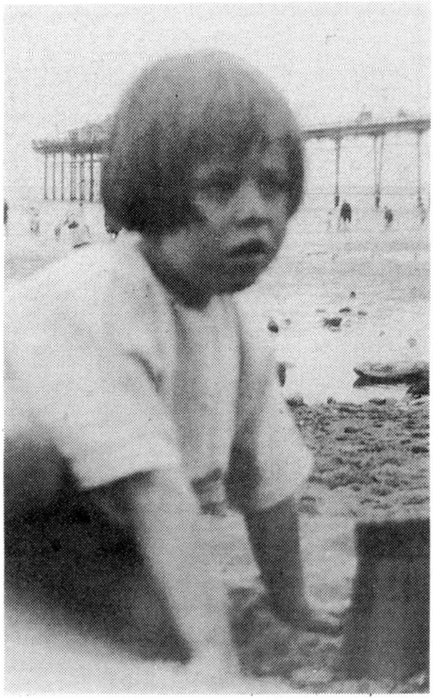

Sandcastles

On winter evenings we loved a sing song round the piano, and especially the choruses from Ira. D. Sankey's *Sacred Songs and Solos*. A favourite was 'Shall we Gather at the River' - in my imagination I saw all our friends and relations in a great gathering by the river on the green in front of the Ferry Boat. My brother's favourite was 'Stand up! Stand up! for Jesus' which is very demanding when accompanied by impromptu actions and marching. One of my 18th century forebears was The Rev. John Newton, Captain of a Slave Trader before his conversion. He is best known today for his 'Amazing Grace', but our singing usually ended in his memory with 'Glorious things of Thee are Spoken'.

I can conjure up still the Churchillian gravel tones of The Rev. J.A. Ross, whose jaws seemed to forget that they were no longer clamped to the tobacco pipe which it was their wont to hold, as his voice intoned from Isaiah Chapter Forty the words 'They shall renew their strength, they shall mount up on wings like eagles, they shall run and not be weary, they shall walk and not faint.' Great words, made especially memorable to a small boy to whom the church lectern in the form of an eagle with outspread wings and mounted on an orb ready for take off, was one of the wonders of his world.

Sunday is really two days in one. A day of 'rest' and re-creation to recuperate from the activity of the preceding week, and a day of preparation for the week to come. To me, Sunday is the first day of the week, although many calendars now print it as the last!

Perhaps, above all, it is a day on which to ponder the meaning of life for *'The fool hath said in his heart, there is no God!'*

'Amazing Grace' by the Rev. John Newton
set to the Ira D. Sankey version

The following words from the poem 'Little Gidding' are engraved on the tomb of T.S. Elliot in Westminster Abbey:

If you come this way,
Taking any route, starting from anywhere,
At any time or any season,
It would always be the same: you would have to put off ,
Sense and notion.
You are not here to verify,
Instruct yourself, or inform curiosity,
Or carry report. You are here to kneel,
Where prayer has been valid. And prayer is more
Than an order of words, the conscious occupation
Of the praying mind, or the sound of the voice praying,
And what the dead had no speech for, when living,
They can tell you, being dead: the communication
Of the dead is tongued with fire beyond the language
of living.

Chapter 29

Steam Ploughs and Runaways

The Fowler steam driven Ploughing Engines were a steam-man's dream come true, but to me they appeared as ugly black monsters - one could hear them a mile away, their great iron wheels grinding on gravel road, and their demanding whistle. They travelled in pairs like prehistoric creatures roaming the countryside looking for good earth to get their teeth in and tear apart. A little man, all important, out front, waving red flags to warn of their approach. I came to dislike them - even to hate them!

Eager to Work, by Joe Godderidge

It was the beginning of the end for noble 'Boxer', for the ever eager 'Smart'. and the long line of gentle Shire horses who, up to the coming of the steam plough, had drawn the shining shares through the arable fields of England for generations, with a little help in earlier times from the Ox.

Our country had depended on the heavy draught horse, particularly the Shire, throughout history. Well into the 1920's there were a million or more of them in the British Isles, of which half were to be destroyed within a few years to make way for mechanisation and the tractor. More than 250,000 were killed during the fighting in the First World War. Increasing mechanisation and the Second World War saw their almost complete removal from the fields. Large numbers were exported for human consumption to the continent.

The Shire Horse was brought over from France to England with the Norman invasion of 1066. Used as war horse they had the strength and stamina to carry a knight fully clad in armour. The English, although using a lighter horse to move about the battle field, fought with battleaxe on foot. The breed was much improved by Robert Bakewell (1725 - 1795), one of the 18th century's great breeders of sheep, cattle and horses.

'Harold' and the Grey Mare, by Goe Godderidge

Soon to be a thing of the past, was the annual sight of the beribboned stallion, proud head held high above his keeper, as he walked the country roads visiting the mares in their season. To be followed in the spring by a new generation of young foals, eager to nuzzle their mothers for that life-giving milk to strengthen wobbly legs which one day would take the strain of many a load in their daily toil.

The spluttering Fordson tractor had not yet puffed out it's sooty fumes into the clean Holywell air - but with the approaching war and the need for increased food production, it would soon do so. However willing, plodding horse and man were soon to be no longer good enough.

The ploughing engine cavalcade was an awe-inspiring sight, rare enough in the early 30's to bring people out of their houses to watch it pass. Men paused in their work to follow its progress along the road. Special permission had to be sought for the engines to pass over the level crossing at Needingworth railway gates, and the track inspected by an L.N.E.R. official to confirm that no damage had been done. In addition to the pair of engines, there was a tip-over four-furrow plough, one or two water tankers, a maintenance van and a living van, all on solid iron wheels. The crew lived and slept with their charges as they moved from farm to farm. The fire boxes were damped down at night, but the fire not extinguished so that steam pressure could quickly be built up with the coming of daylight.

Horses had been known to shy and bolt at the sight and sound of these monsters, as the begrimed driver's mates smashed and shovelled yet more of the hard black engine coal into their gaping mouths. Each farm had several tons of this shining coal ready and waiting for their arrival. Escaping steam, hissing in jets as the regulators kept the pressure steady, and clouds of black tar laden smoke were chuffed out to smart the eyes of onlookers.

There was an air of excitement as steady progress was made to the village, and on through Needingworth and Mill Way to the thirty acres of arable land ideally situated for this type of cultivation. The engines would take up station at either side of the field and, by means of a steel hawser, draw the plough through the soil, then tip it over and back again, the shining shares going back and forth until the job was done.

A signalling system of short and long blasts on the steam whistle provided communication between the drivers who had great skill in controlling their charges, often out of sight of each other due to the rise and fall of the land. Elephant trunk-like hoses hung in the water tankers, sucked them dry and called for more: No hedgerow well could replenish itself from the gravel bed at the rate needed to fill the tankers which moved first to one and then to the other engine.

'Out of the way boy; if that hawser breaks it will have your head off as clean as a whistle.' So it was to the river for water, and no let-up. The river was a good mile away across the pasture land, up the lane, and by way of the village to the old ferry crossing place, where a steady slope gave space for horses to stand and drink while the hand pump was plied back and forth until the tank was full.

On a clear bright day with frost on the ground, ploughing conditions would be ideal and the monsters would shout in panic for water. With steam pressure at danger point, and no water, the boiler could crack or burst, so there was much swearing on the odd occasion when the fire had to be damped down and ploughing brought to a standstill. Just now and again there would be time for Bolcher to take a quick pint at the Ferry Boat Inn.

'The Hill', Holywell, by W.F. Garden

One day we had Smart, a young and impetuous horse, in the shafts of the tanker and Beauty harnessed in the lead. In this way, on tight harness, Smart could use his boundless energy in taking the pull of the load and Beauty with her experience could regulate the speed. Now, along the front of the village there is a slope leading from the higher ground to the fen level. It could hardly be called a hill although as such it was known. It had been freshly gravelled to make better purchase for the wheels as the tanker returned fully laden from the river. Bolcher was driving the pair, and he and I were standing side by side on the backboard of the shafts, leaning with our backs against the smooth round end of the tank - never an easy ride with the shafts moving about as the horses plodded along.

The smooth iron wheels were crunching on the gravel. Bolcher was encouraging the pair to take it steady as we approached the downwards slope of the hill. 'Steady now', 'Hold back me beauties', 'Whoa there Smart'. Meanwhile holding back on the reins, but it was no good, however tight the pull on the reins, the slithering of the wheels on the gravel and pressure of weight from behind caused Smart to push into the backside of Beauty who was trying to hold back. Neither could do so, and against urgent cries of 'Whoa-whoa there' Beauty had had enough of Smart pressing against her rump and they were-off - bolting in a nightmare race for the river. Bolcher was thrown straight away - he had been gripping the reins with both hands. As he fell beneath the lurching tanker he shouted, 'Jump Boy, Jump', but I could not jump. With one hand tight on the water pump handle, legs going up and down as the shafts rose crazily up and down, I was too scared to jump and leant back hard against the tank. We careered along the road, nearside wheel bouncing on and off the grass verge, at a bend in the road the tanker almost capsized but righted itself with no slackening of pace. Nearly thrown myself, but holding fast we raced toward the river. Panic now gripped me and I was about to jump as I had no wish to drown, when suddenly the offside wheel caught a drainage rut and I was catapulted through the air to land with a thud on the river bank - bruised but with no bones broken. 'I thought you was a gonner there, boy' I heard a voice say as I came to my senses. It was Tom Metcalf who had watched the episode toward the end, and had shouted 'Hold on, hold on, they'll stop in the river'. That is just what they did quivering but fortunately unhurt. Miraculously, the tanker had remained upright.

The Ferryboat Inn at Holywell

I limped back along the road, to find Bolcher on his feet but in agony from his leg where the iron wheel had run over his knee. It mended, but he never got the full use back into that leg and ever after walked with a limp.

That was the end of riding the tanker for me. Do you wonder I disliked the steam cultivators! Theirs was to be but a brief appearance on the changing scene of agriculture. Soon to be a thing of the past, and like the dinosaur which once roamed this land, destined to become museum pieces to be looked at in wonder.

Soon it was to be the age of the tractor, in its many shapes and sizes, from the little grey Ferguson to the giant crawler.

Who knows, the day of the Shire horse may yet come again!

Chapter 30

Gypsies

Life is sweet, brother;
There's night and day,
both sweet things;
The sun, moon and the stars,
brother, all sweet things.
There's likewise a wind on the heath,
who would wish to die?
Lavengro; George Borrow

The Gipsy Encampment, by A. Austen

To those who are not country folk the word Gypsy conjures up pictures of gaily painted caravans and blue smoke drifting from a camp fire; Flamenco dancers whirling with clicking fingers, or Hungarian violins playing some romantic melody. That is as may be, but to me the mention of Gypsy brings to life once more both sad and happy memories of the Smith family.

They came one day from 'out Bedford way' and my father allowed them to set up camp in Brownlow's field off the Needingworth Road. The head of the family was Shadrach Smith, known as 'old Shady' (misconstrued locally as of shady character), his wife was simply known as 'the old lady', and they had three children; Tom the eldest, Belinda with long raven black hair and freckles, and Bob (also Shadrach) the youngest. The family was descended from true

Shadrach Smith, 'Old Shady'

Romany stock and hated the term Diddecoy as they were sometimes called by those who knew no better.

Dark of complexion, husky voiced, they lived in igloo-shaped structures; tents would be too fine a word. Constructed from supple willow poles, sometimes split, and bent toward the centre, covered with brushwood woven in, and any old bits of tarpaulin or carpet, anything that would help keep out the rain. From the largest of these structures, of which the number varied, there led out two or three small individual sleeping quarters. Family washing was laid out to dry on the sloe bushes. The camp was always tidy - not the scrap metal and rubbish-strewn camp site of the Diddecoys.

In return for being allowed to stay in the field they kept the cattle water trough filled daily from a well in the hedgerow, and no doubt

Tom Smith, Shady's elder son

this was convenient for their own use. The water was drawn up in an old bucket on a rope There was no nitrate trouble in those days. It was quite common for there to be a well in the hedgerow of a field, used for grazing cattle, most of them were well hidden and their location known to very few people. The Smith's kept an eye on the cattle and on any would-be trespassers.

There was an occasion when Tom was sent running, over the railway track, by the old ballast hole, down Parson's Drove by the brook, over the foot-bridge and up Conger Lane to the Manor. Legs stung by nettle and scratched by briar to bring news that the recently built hayrick was smouldering. Had it not been for this timely word it would probably have fired; a wedge was soon cut out of the centre and the hay saved. Hayricks are prone to combustion if the state of the hay is misjudged at the time of stacking. Judging the right time to cut the hay crop is always a chancy business even today with sophisticated weather forecasting. There is nothing more satisfying to a dairy farmer than a good crop of sweet smelling hay.

Sometimes my father, who the Smiths would address as 'Mussa Nole', would stop for a chat when passing or calling to check the cattle; given the chance I would sit by the fire and listen to the talk, always about country matters and in a brogue so different from our local voices. My father still had some of the soft Oxfordshire burr tones in his voice. They were an honest and hardworking family, but what a hard and miserable way to live, especially in the winter. Many years later, good-intentioned authorities put Mrs. Shady and Belinda in an old railway crossing gate keeper's cottage, but they could not stand the claustrophobia of the four walls and soon moved out again to live under the open sky.

It was a joy, and an excitement to a small boy to see old Shady driving his piebald pony in its flat-bottomed cart with the family aboard and their lurcher dog running alongside, on their way to the day's work at Holywell or elsewhere, whereever work was to be found according to the season: Perhaps singling sugar beet and hoeing the crop, almost always done on a piecework basis and paid by acreage or by the row. Picking french beans (by the 14 lb net) for canning by Chivers at their Huntingdon factory; and gooseberries, strawberries, apples, all in their turn. Occasionally, Mrs Shady would have to bring the boys to order, when work got tiresome so that pelting one another with clods of earth, or playing with the dog, became more attractive.

I've seen Tom riding the piebald by standing on its hind quarters, arms outstretched - a sight which would otherwise need a visit to Bertram Mills Circus. The excitement those circus posters caused in the village!

To see them wrapped round a telegraph pole, or in the window of the White Horse public house, was nearly as good, and usually as much as we got of the circus itself. On the high road, Bob could ride his bike one foot on the saddle and one on the cross bar. Not an easy trick and one which usually ended in disaster and laughter as the speed dropped away.

Once, the labour exchange sent some men to help pick the beans. It was the nearest thing we ever came to strike or a fight by the Smiths. There was some right on their side. The newcomers had no long term interest in the crop, pulling many plants up by the root, trampling on others, or picking beans not yet ready. They probably did not want

Lifting Sugar Beet, by Joe Godderidge

the job anyway, and were quite happy to know that their services were no longer required. The labour exchange was not called upon again, and it became a matter of honour to the gypsies to get the crop harvested.

When my father gave up Brownlow's field, the Smith family moved to another field at the top of Lowndes Drove. Here there was an old barn which no doubt came in useful in inclement weather, although it had to be shared with young heifers or bullocks.

When there was no other work to be done Mrs. Smith would go round with the basket. Shady made clothes pegs by the dozen as he sat by the fire, two pieces of willow stick whittled to shape and held firmly together by a small strip of metal cut from an old baked bean tin and secured by a small nail. Housewives often preferred them to the dollypeg, being less liable to break. She also had coloured ribbon, bits of lace, and reels of cotton; anything to make a few pence. Old Mrs. Shady never went in for fortune telling, at least not at our house, although Esmeralda, one of her relatives, would sometimes do so.

In the spring they would pick dog daisies from the embankment of the railway cutting where they grew in abundance, and either sell them from the basket in St. Ives, or send them off to market through the local agent, Cecil Prior (known as the midnight milkman, but that is another story).

With the passage of time and after my mother had given up the farm, the old lady would visit us from time to time on a Saturday; standing by the kitchen door in her clean white apron - never coming in unless to shelter from a passing storm, and then only to stand on the mat. She would enjoy a cup of tea and a slice of bread and dripping. Often taking a pot of dripping home for 'my Linda'.

I still have the cup, breakfast size, handle now broken, but the scarlet pimpernel decoration she loved as bright as ever. Reminding her of the bright eyed scarlet pimpernels of the harvest field. 'They was luvly in the wheat, Mussa Joey' - always commented upon.

The 20's and 30's were the good years for the Smiths. In the fullness of time, tuberculosis, diabetes, and the rigours of their way of life took their toll, until Belinda alone was left to live out a lonely life with her bantams in a caravan at Needingworth. After her mother died Belinda rarely missed cycling or walking to Somersham on a Saturday to lay a flower on her mother's grave - such is love born of adversity.

I saw Belinda laid to rest in Somersham churchyard, to the sound of wind in a driving rain. It was fitting music, in farewell of a gypsy girl.

It was a sad day!

Chapter 31

The Uncertainty of Life

"Enjoy the spring of love and youth,
To some good angel leave the rest,
For time will teach thee soon the truth,
There are no birds' in last year's nest."

Anon

Such is the transient and uncertain nature of life, that between the rising of the sun in the morning and the going down of the same, an unexpected event can have an immediate and lasting effect on the whole future. One such event took place shortly after my eleventh birthday.

It was a cold January day with snow on the ground and ice for sliding on the pond. We were enjoying our dinner of lamb stew with swede and dumplings. On such days the smallest detail is imprinted on the mind. My father had been persuaded to remain in his bed - having received severe bruising a few days earlier when a sick horse, being turned for its comfort, had rolled upon him. A cart horse weighs in the region of a ton! As the meal progressed my mother took a cup of tea up to his bedroom, and returning a few minutes later said in a matter of fact tone of voice 'Your father has just died'.

'We will say the Lord's Prayer - then finish your dinner - we shall all need strength for the coming days'. I now know that this composure was but an expedient to meet the need of the hour.

Earlier in the day I had been called to the room where my father was writing cheques, and given instruction for their delivery. One of them was to Harry Anderson for work done by his steam cultivators, and another to Standen's for shoeing the horses. On delivering the cheque to Mr. Anderson at Westwood Farm, St. Ives I was given half a crown, so I was pleased, and my father too, on being told of it upon my return home. He asked me to read to him the 23rd Psalm 'The Lord is my Shepherd, I shall not want', and then some lines from Elizabeth Wetherell's classic story 'The Wide Wide World'. This was the very first of the few books he had possessed in his youth and remained his favourite throughout life, so I believe he had a premonition that his work on earth was done and a new life was about to begin.

After the meal I was sent on my bicycle to Needingworth to the home of Rose Mansfield with the most cryptic, yet meaningful, message I ever carried, 'Ask Rose to please come, and bring a pair of white socks'.

He was carried to his grave by the men who had worked alongside him on the farm, and an era was over.

These same men were loyal to his memory and to my mother, and the day-to-day running of the farm continued as the seasons determined. Cows were milked, hay made, the soil cultivated, pigs sent to market. It so happened that two days after the death of my father, a similar fate befell my Uncle Erastus Watts, a corn miller, of Hemingford Grey. He succumbed to a heart attack whilst grinding some barley on a bitterly cold day, 23rd January 1933. But for this tragedy, he would have been of assistance to my mother in running the farm at Holywell.

Farming in the 1930's was in a state of depression, brought about largely by the government having gone back on its promise to maintain the price of grain. Corn prices dropped to below twenty per cent and farmers went into bankruptcy or got into debt to the bank. Dairy farmers relied on the milk cheque to pay the wages, and sometimes it was not sufficient. As a child, I was only vaguely aware of these difficulties by overhearing adult conversation at home or at market.

Eventually, Manor Farm was once again put up for sale, and on 27th March 1935, Farmers! Bargain Hunters!, and interested on-lookers gathered at the farm for the unreserved dispersal sale of live and dead farm stock. Irrespective of the reason for such sales, and there is usually an implicit tragedy, either human or financial, the day has a festive air as friends meet and chat, and grumble about the weather and the government, both of which are held responsible for most of a farmer's woes.

There was a hum of expectancy as the ringing of the bell, an 'honour' given to my brother Henry, announced the commencement of the sale. The voice of Cyril Watts, Auctioneer of St. Ives, and friend of my late father, called the gathering to order.

The livestock were paraded one by one for inspection, prodded with ash stick, and to the fall of the gavel on the rostrum, found themselves for good or ill in the care of a new owner. Farm machinery, tackle, and domestic equipment of all kinds were loaded up on cart and lorry, or towed away until, as the catalogue stated, all were dispersed, and an eerie silence settled over the farmstead.

27th March, 1935. Without Reserve.

THE MANOR FARM, HOLYWELL,

NEAR ST. IVES, HUNTS.

Catalogue of Unreserved Dispersal Sale of the whole of the Live and Dead

FARM STOCK

including

THE HERD OF

36 DAIRY COWS & HEIFERS

Bull and 14 Head of Young Stock

10 HORSES

3 Sows and Litters, 40 Strong Store Pigs,

POULTRY AND 5 GEESE,

THE IMPLEMENTS, MACHINES,

Carts, Harness, Barn Tackle, Poultry Houses, Dairy Utensils and other Effects

WHICH

MR. CYRIL WATTS

Has been instructed by MRS. NEWELL (who has sold the Farm), to Sell by Auction, on

WEDNESDAY, 27th MARCH, 1935

Commencing at **11 o'clock** prompt.

Refreshments will be provided.

Catalogues may be obtained of the Auctioneer, St. Ives.
Telephone No. 11.

DARLOW, PRINTER, FREE CHURCH PASSAGE, ST. IVES.

All the familiar sounds were gone. No more could be heard the rattling of old Tom's chain on the manger edge, no whinnying from the stable, no blaring of calves calling their mothers, no contented grunts from the piggery, no shouts or ribald remarks between tired men as they made their way home after the day's work. The rhythmic clip-clopping of Kim's hooves as she carried Bill homeward in the trap to wife and family, no more faded into the distance. The gates were chained and doors locked. All was emptiness.

Throughout its history the Manor had resounded to the cries of nature and laughter of children. This stillness was not the end but a pause, until a new family would loose the chains and unlock the doors. Then the old familiar sounds would return, and a new story with new characters would begin to unfold in a new age.

I wonder would they feel the magic and come to love this place as I had done?

I hope so.

The Fraser Family Tree

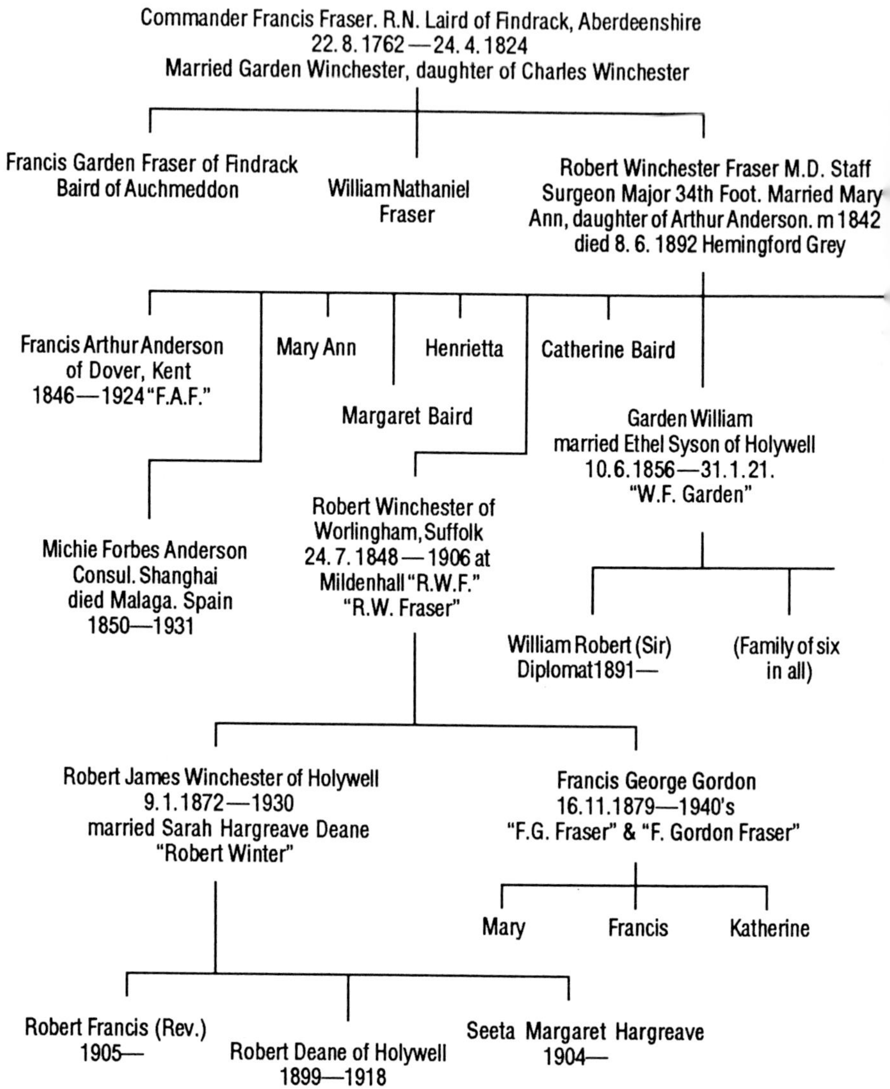

For clarity the FRASER surname has been omitted from the tree after that of Robert James Winchester Fraser M.D.

Commander Fraser was a descendant of the Lord High Chamberlain of Scotland and his wife Mary, sister of Robert Bruce.
The family crest is a Stag's Head with the motto
'Je Suis Prest' — 'I am ready'

George Gordon
11.4.1859—1895
married in 1884
at Larne, Ireland.
Catherine Home
Ramsey Ross
"George Gordon Fraser"
"G.G. Fraser'

Arthur Anderson of Holywell
20.12.1861—2.3.1904
married Margaret Elizabeth 1863
—d 9.1.47
"A. Fraser", "A.F",
"A.A.", "A.A.F."

Gilbert Baird of Holywell
23.7.1866—6.2.1947
married 24.8.1897
May Heseltine
(Great Aunt of
Michael Heseltine M.P.)
"G. Baird" & "G Baird Fraser"

Francis Mc Greigor of Holywell
31.3.1866—25.2.1930

Alistair Hay 2nd. Lt. 41 Sqdn. R.A.F
2.8.1894—11.8.1918
(of wounds in France)

Mary Theresa Henrietta Dorothy
27.5.1899—3.3.21

Helen Baird Clementine Dibdin
1.6.06—15.10.73
m. Dr. William S. Grove

Rupert Baird Andrew
7.11.09—2.3.74

William Andrew Baird Grove b. 27. 4. 43
m. Rosalind Hilary Callan b. 15. 8. 45

Margaret May Fraser Grove
b. 25. 3. 48 married Robert McNab

William Roy
b. 15. 5. 74

Antonia Louise
b. 29. 8. 79

Alexander Dominic
b. 20. 7. 84

Sophia Marianne
b. 18. 1. 89

Nicola Clare
b. 2. 7. 72

James Robert Winchester McNab
b. 2. 2. 83

Ruth Mary Cardall McNab
b. 25. 3. 85

Aerial view of Holywell 1982

Holywell-cum-Needingworth 1902

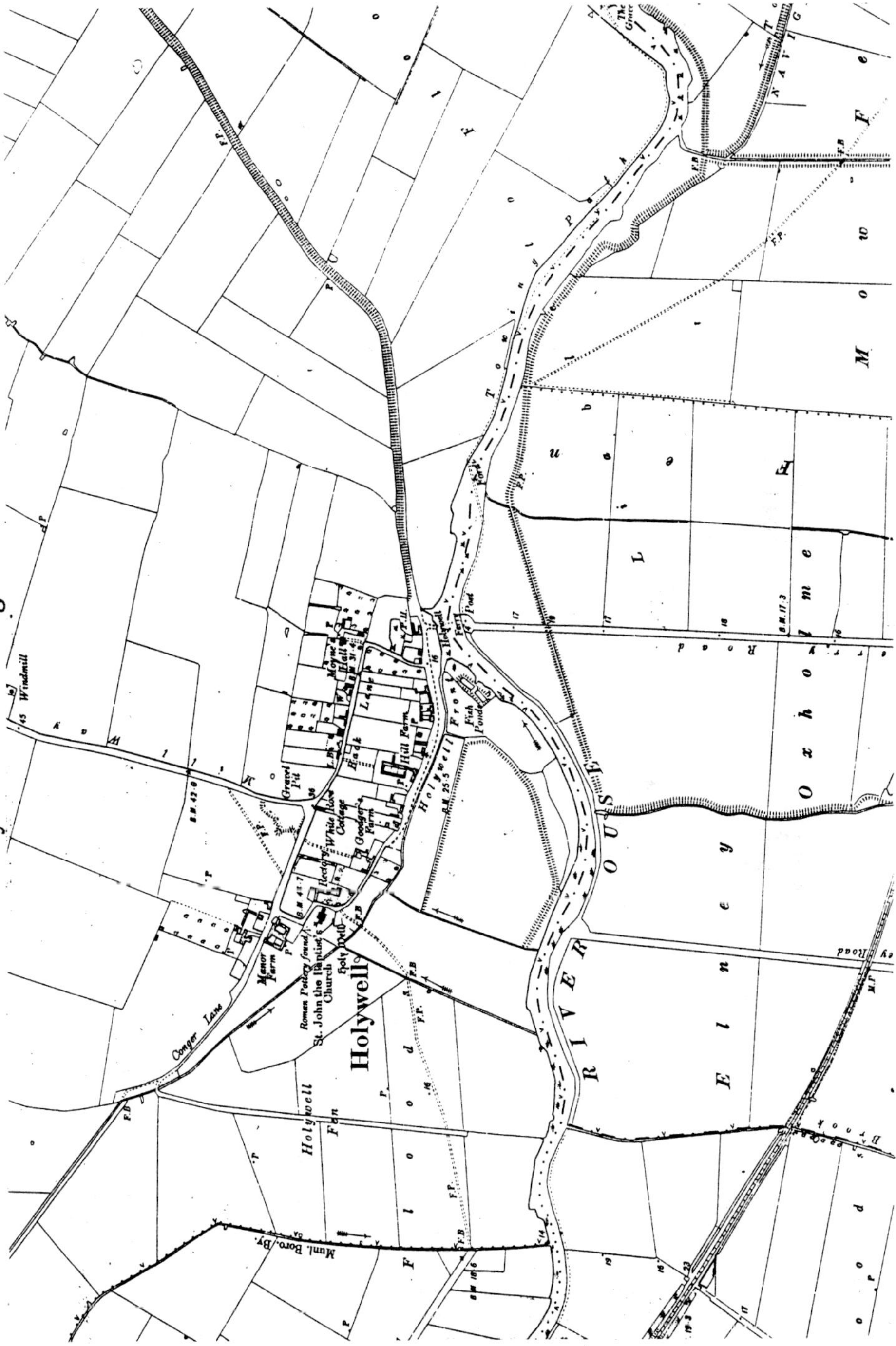

Holywell-cum-Needingworth The Parish Church of St. John the Baptist

Date	Rectors	Resigned or Deceased
C. 990	Gode	-
1216	Robert Morrell (King's Clerk)	-
1221	Roger	-
1240	Peter of York	-
1247	Ralph of Ramsey	-
-	Hugo de Botiler	d1308
1308	William de Loriaco	d1311
1311	Theobald de Troyes	r1311
1311	Guerin de Tilleris	cess1318
1318	Stephen D'Albini	ex1320
1320	Roger de Clisseby	-
-	Peter le Vavasour	here1324
1325	John de Colonia	ex1335
1335	William Drax	d1349
1349	Thomas Powis or Prior M.A.	
	(Warden of King's Hall,Camb.)	d1361
1362	Walter d'aldeby. B.C.L.	
	(Prebend of Winchester)	d1375
1375	John de Seynesbury	-
1377	John Morice	here1392
1392	Thomas de Wigetoft (King's Clerk)	-
1403	William Lassels LL.B.	
-	(Archdeacon of Huntingdon 1421-63	
-	Chanc. Camb. University 1431-2)	r1407
1407	Richard Brayton	-
1408	Robert Claydon	-
1420	Thos Pulter B.A. (Prebend of Lichfield)	r1403
1423	William Dallyng. D. Can.L.	
	(Master of Trinity Hall,	
	Camb 1471-1500)	d1500
1501	Walter Hewke D.Can.L.	
	(Master of Trinity Hall 1512-1517)	d1517
1518	John Nevyll B.C.L.	-
1535	John Dromyng B.A.	d1543
1544	John Fyley	d1554

Date	Rectors	Resigned or Deceased
1555	William Downham D.D. (Chaplain to the Princess Elizabeth 1548. Bishop of Chester 1561-77)	r1561
1561	John Bridgewater, M.A. (Archdeacon of Rochester 1560)	-
1569	John Welles, M.A. (Fellow of Kings Coll Cambridge.)	d1570
1570	William Chaderton D.D. (Bishop of Chester 1579-95 Bishop of Lincoln 1595-1608)	cess1579
1579	Bartholomew Chamberlain, D.D.	r1601
1602	Noah Bowier, M.A.	d1645
1646	Francis Wilford D.D. (Dean of Ely 1662-67)	d1667
1667	Thos. Tenison D.D. (Bishop of Lincoln 1692-5 Archbishop of Canterbury 1695-1715)	cess1681
1681	John Knighton, D.D. (Prebend of Lincoln)	d1703
1704	Alexander Torriano D.C.L. (Prebend of Lincoln)	d1717
1717	Thomas Collins B.A	d1722
1722	Henry Parratt, B.A. (Prebend of Lincoln)	d1757
1757	Thomas Lydiatt, LL.B.	d1761
1761	Matthew Maddock M.A. (Fellow of Brasenose Coll. Oxford)	d1788
1788	Benjamin Hutchinson F.R.S. (Preb. of Lincoln)	d1804
1804	William James Aislabie, M.A.	d1843
1843	Samuel Boydell Beckwith, B.A.	d1846
1846	Robert James McGhee, M.A.	d1872
1872	Charles Henry Williams Hoskyns, M.A.	d1893
1893	Edward Norgate, B.A.	r1909
1909	John Frederick Tanfield, M.A	cess1913
1914	James Alfred Ross, M.A.	d1945
1946	Alex. Geo. McLennan Pearce Higgins, M.A.	1960
1960	F. Bateman	1965
1965	Rev. E. Edgehill	1968
1969	Rev. Hugh Pettingell	r1971
1971	Rev. C.S. Jerome	1978
1980	Rev. J. Wilcox L. Th.	r1986
1987	Rev. Owen Swan	